HIP HOP
Goes Science
Volume I

VASILEIOS YFANTIS

DEDICATION

I would like to dedicate this book to all the scholars of popular music that explore the hidden side of the genres by focusing on the unknown elements on musical and cultural level.

CONTENTS

ACKNOWLEDGMENTS

I would like to thanks the University of West Attica for their help towards
my research by allowing me to use their resources for the access to
academic records relevant to the hip hop culture and music.

PROLOGUE

The music genre of hip hop was developed in US during the 1970s by African Americans and Latino Americans. Nowadays, the hip hop is a global phenomenon on musical and cultural level by expanding its impact on other types of art such as painting, poetry and other forms.

Hip hop is a popular phenomenon and most of the fans tend to view it from the listener's perspective including the recorded samples, loops, beats, rhymes and the other musical parts. However, I strongly believe that hip hop is more than a sequence of notes, beats, sporty clothing and a larger than life image. This is the accurate scope of this book, to provide the hip hop fan with the knowledge about the other side of hip hop.

The other side of hip hop from my point of view, is the scientific usage of hip hop as an academic tool to teach science or as a separate academic area. Have you ever thought that hip hop music and culture could be more than a soundtrack for dance and to have a good time? Read between the lines and think how you can use hip hop to discuss through its lyrics about sociology, music technology and even history. An average teacher divides the delivered knowledge of the academic time into separate lectures. If each lecture adopts hip hop elements as a "content trigger" to draw the students' interest in learning then we have something that worth discussion. Additionally, hip hop could be a separate academic area since it has an academic status through its presence in thousands of academic writings, yes thousands! Volume I of this research presents only a part of the academic writings that use hip hop as an academic tool, or explore the genre as a scientific phenomenon.

The current book is a bibliographic guide about the academic use of hip hop between 1988 and 2009 with a presentation of the most important academic writings about hip hop. If you really want to read about the science in or through hip hop, then use this book as a guide to lead you into knowledge. Even if you have less time for reading, by owning this book you can prove to the "outsiders" that the ongoing success of hip hop lies in the fact that it is a serious subject for discussion. The title of this book: "Hip hop Goes Science" is also a life statement that hip hop can go science and should be treated seriously, away from clichés and social norms about its risky effects. Can you consider negative influence, a music genre that has been active since the 1970s and is adopted by the educators as a tool? I guess not... Hip hop goes science and here is the Volume I of all the scientific works that prove its scientific value...

Callard, S.
Music TV dances to a new rhythm
(1999) Cable and Satellite Europe, 0 (189), p. 24.
LANGUAGE OF ORIGINAL DOCUMENT: English
DOCUMENT TYPE: Article

Dimitriadis, G.
Hip hop to rap: Some implications of an historically situated approach to performance
(1999) Text and Performance Quarterly, 19 (4), pp. 355-369.
LANGUAGE OF ORIGINAL DOCUMENT: English
DOCUMENT TYPE: Article

Bennett, A.
Rappin' on the tyne: White hip hop culture in northeast England - An ethnographic study
(1999) Sociological Review, 47 (1), pp. X-24.
PUBLISHER: Blackwell Publishing Ltd
LANGUAGE OF ORIGINAL DOCUMENT: English
DOCUMENT TYPE: Article

McLeod, K.
Authenticity within hip-hop and other cultures threatened with assimilation
(1999) Journal of Communication, 49 (4), pp. 134-150.
PUBLISHER: Oxford University Press
LANGUAGE OF ORIGINAL DOCUMENT: English
DOCUMENT TYPE: Article

Ibrahim, A.E.K.M.
Becoming black: Rap and hip-hop, race, gender, identity, and the politics of ESL learning
(1999) TESOL Quarterly, 33 (3), pp. 349-369.

PUBLISHER: Wiley Blackwell
LANGUAGE OF ORIGINAL DOCUMENT: English
DOCUMENT TYPE: Article

Hernandez, D.P., Garofalo, R.
Deborah pacini hernandez and reebee garofalo: Hip hop in havana rap, race and national identity in contemporary cuba
(1999) Journal of Popular Music Studies, 11-12 (1), pp. 18-47.
LANGUAGE OF ORIGINAL DOCUMENT: English
DOCUMENT TYPE: Article

Hutchinson, J.F.
The hip hop generation: African American male-female relationships in a nightclub setting
(1999) Journal of Black Studies, 30 (1), pp. 62-84.
PUBLISHER: SAGE Publications Inc.
LANGUAGE OF ORIGINAL DOCUMENT: English
DOCUMENT TYPE: Article

Ogbar, J.O.G.
Slouching toward bork. The culture wars and self-criticism in hip-hop music
(1999) Journal of Black Studies, 30 (2), pp. 164-183.
PUBLISHER: SAGE Publications Inc.
LANGUAGE OF ORIGINAL DOCUMENT: English
DOCUMENT TYPE: Article

Bennett, A.
Hip hop am main: The localization of rap music and hip hop culture
(1999) Media, Culture and Society, 21 (1), pp. 77-91.
PUBLISHER: SAGE Publications Ltd
LANGUAGE OF ORIGINAL DOCUMENT: English
DOCUMENT TYPE: Article

Aparicio, F.R.
The blackness of sugar: Celia cruz and the performance of (trans)nationalism

(1999) Cultural Studies, 13 (2), pp. 223-236.
PUBLISHER: Routledge
LANGUAGE OF ORIGINAL DOCUMENT: English
DOCUMENT TYPE: Article

Prévos, A.J.M.
Hip-hop, rap, and repression in France and in the United States
(1998) Popular Music and Society, 22 (2), pp. 67-84.
LANGUAGE OF ORIGINAL DOCUMENT: English
DOCUMENT TYPE: Article

Elflein, D.
From Krauts with attitudes to Turks with attitudes: Some aspects of hip-hop history in Germany
(1998) Popular Music, 17 (3), pp. 255-265.
LANGUAGE OF ORIGINAL DOCUMENT: English
DOCUMENT TYPE: Review

Kotarba, J.A.
Black men, black voices: The role of the producer in synthetic performance ethnography
(1998) Qualitative Inquiry, 4 (3), pp. 389-404.
LANGUAGE OF ORIGINAL DOCUMENT: English
DOCUMENT TYPE: Article

Stephens, T., Braithwaite, R.L., Taylor, S.E.
Model for using hip-hop music for small group HIV/AIDS prevention counseling with African American adolescents and young adults
(1998) Patient Education and Counseling, 35 (2), pp. 127-137.

PUBLISHER: Elsevier Ireland Ltd
LANGUAGE OF ORIGINAL DOCUMENT: English
DOCUMENT TYPE: Article

Stapleton, K.R.
From the margins to mainstream: The political power of hip-hop
(1998) Media, Culture and Society, 20 (2), pp. 219-234.
PUBLISHER: SAGE Publications Ltd
LANGUAGE OF ORIGINAL DOCUMENT: English
DOCUMENT TYPE: Article

Caglar, A.S.
Popular culture, marginality and institutional incorporation german-turkish rap and turkish pop in Berlin
(1998) Cultural Dynamics, 10 (3), pp. 243-261.
PUBLISHER: SAGE Publications Ltd
LANGUAGE OF ORIGINAL DOCUMENT: English
DOCUMENT TYPE: Article

Ferrell, J.
Freight train Graffiti: Subculture, crime, dislocation
(1998) Justice Quarterly, 15 (4), pp. X-608.
PUBLISHER: Routledge

LANGUAGE OF ORIGINAL DOCUMENT: English
DOCUMENT TYPE: Article

Martin, R.
The composite body: Hip-hop aerobics and the multicultural nation
(1997) Journal of Sport and Social Issues, 21 (2), pp. 120-133.
LANGUAGE OF ORIGINAL DOCUMENT: English
DOCUMENT TYPE: Article

Frydman, J., Höhfeld, J.
Chaperones get in touch: The Hip-Hop connection
(1997) Trends in Biochemical Sciences, 22 (3), pp. 87-92.
LANGUAGE OF ORIGINAL DOCUMENT: English
DOCUMENT TYPE: Review

Maxwell, I.
Hip hop aesthetics and the will to culture1
(1997) Australian Journal of Anthropology, 8 (2), pp. 50-70.
LANGUAGE OF ORIGINAL DOCUMENT: English
DOCUMENT TYPE: Article

Jones, K.
Are rap videos more violent? Style differences and the prevalence of sex and violence in the age of MTV
(1997) Howard Journal of Communications, 8 (4), pp. 343-356.
LANGUAGE OF ORIGINAL DOCUMENT: English
DOCUMENT TYPE: Article

Barber-Kersovan, A.
Street noise: A hip-hop project considering unemployment
(1997) Journal of Popular Music Studies, 9-10 (1), pp. 7-19.
LANGUAGE OF ORIGINAL DOCUMENT: English
DOCUMENT TYPE: Article

Smitherman, G.
"The Chain Remain the Same" Communicative Practices in the

Hip Hop Nation
(1997) Journal of Black Studies, 28 (1), pp. 3-25.
LANGUAGE OF ORIGINAL DOCUMENT: English
DOCUMENT TYPE: Article

Smith, C.H.
Method in the madness: Exploring the boundaries of identity in hip-hop performativity
(1997) Social Identities, 3 (3), pp. 345-374.
PUBLISHER: Carfax Publishing Company
LANGUAGE OF ORIGINAL DOCUMENT: English
DOCUMENT TYPE: Article

Dimitriadis, G.
Hip hop: From live performance to mediated narrative
(1996) Popular Music, 15 (2), pp. 179-194.
LANGUAGE OF ORIGINAL DOCUMENT: English
DOCUMENT TYPE: Review

McMillen, L.
'Hip-hop intellectual': Cultural-studies scholar Michael Eric Dyson is a lightning rod for controversy
(1996) Chronicle of Higher Education, 42 (20), pp. A6.
LANGUAGE OF ORIGINAL DOCUMENT: English
DOCUMENT TYPE: Article

Mitchell, T.
Questions of Style: Notes on Italian Hip Hop
(1995) Popular Music, 14 (3), pp. 333-348.
LANGUAGE OF ORIGINAL DOCUMENT: English
DOCUMENT TYPE: Article

Tokaji, A.
The Meeting of Sacred and Profane in New York's Music: Robert Moses, Lincoln Center, and Hip-hop
(1995) Journal of American Studies, 29 (1), pp. 97-103.
LANGUAGE OF ORIGINAL DOCUMENT: English
DOCUMENT TYPE: Note

Yancy, G.
Twisted tales: In the hip hop streets of philly
(1995) Popular Music and Society, 19 (3), pp. 131-136.
LANGUAGE OF ORIGINAL DOCUMENT: English
DOCUMENT TYPE: Article

Fenster, M.
Understanding and incorporating rap: The articulation of alternative popular musical practices within dominant cultural practices and institutions
(1995) Howard Journal of Communications, 5 (3), pp. 223-244.
LANGUAGE OF ORIGINAL DOCUMENT: English
DOCUMENT TYPE: Article

Sussman, S., Parker, V.C., Lopes, C., Crippens, D.L., Elder, P., Scholl, D.
Empirical development of brief smoking prevention videotapes which target african-american adolescents
(1995) Substance Use and Misuse, 30 (9), pp. 1141-1164.
PUBLISHER: Informa Healthcare
LANGUAGE OF ORIGINAL DOCUMENT: English
DOCUMENT TYPE: Article

Maxwell, I., Bambrick, N.
Discourses of culture and nationalism in contemporary Sydney hip hop
(1994) Perfect Beat, 2 (1), pp. 1-19.
PUBLISHER: Equinox Publishing Ltd
LANGUAGE OF ORIGINAL DOCUMENT: English
DOCUMENT TYPE: Article

Maxwell, I.
True to the Music: Authenticity, Articulation and Authorship in Sydney Hip Hop Culture
(1994) Social Semiotics, 4 (1-2), pp. 117-137.
LANGUAGE OF ORIGINAL DOCUMENT: English
DOCUMENT TYPE: Article

Sudres, J.-L., Delvert, M., Fouraste, R., Rue, G., Moron, P.
Tag-graffiti: A rehabilitation of youth images. A psycho-social, psycho-clinical and cultural analysis of graffiti [TAG-GRAF: UNE RESTAURATION DES IMAGES ADOLESCENTES? ANALYSE CLINIQUE, PSYCHO-SOCIALE ET CULTURELLE DES GRAFFITI]
(1994) Psychologie Medicale, 26 (8), pp. 736-744.
LANGUAGE OF ORIGINAL DOCUMENT: French
DOCUMENT TYPE: Conference Paper

Burrus, O.
Hip! Hop! Public health [Hip! Hop! La santé publique.]
(1992) Revue de l'"infirmiere, 42 (11), pp. 20-21.
LANGUAGE OF ORIGINAL DOCUMENT: French
DOCUMENT TYPE: Article

Spencer, J.M.
Rapsody in black: Utopian aspirations
(1992) Theology Today, 48 (4), pp. 444-451.
LANGUAGE OF ORIGINAL DOCUMENT: English
DOCUMENT TYPE: Article

Hip hop in minor op
(1991) The Lancet, 338 (8764), p. 441.

LANGUAGE OF ORIGINAL DOCUMENT: English
DOCUMENT TYPE: Note

Brewer, D.D., Miller, M.L.
Bombing and burning: The social organization and values of hip hop graffiti writers and implications for policy
(1990) Deviant Behavior, 11 (4), pp. 345-369.
LANGUAGE OF ORIGINAL DOCUMENT: English
DOCUMENT TYPE: Article

Holmes, S.H.
Hip hop meets winnie mandela
(1988) Black Scholar, 19 (4-5), p. 82.
LANGUAGE OF ORIGINAL DOCUMENT: English
DOCUMENT TYPE: Article

Joseph, C.
Hip hop meets winnie mandela
(1988) Black Scholar, 19 (4-5), p. 83.
LANGUAGE OF ORIGINAL DOCUMENT: English
DOCUMENT TYPE: Article

PUBLICATIONS 2000 - 2009

King, A., Shaw, T., Spence, L.
Hype, hip-hop, and heartbreak: The rise and fall of Kwame Kilpatrick
(2009) Whose Black Politics?: Cases in Post-Racial Black Leadership, pp. 105-129.
PUBLISHER: Routledge
LANGUAGE OF ORIGINAL DOCUMENT: English
DOCUMENT TYPE: Book Chapter

Let the world listen right: The Mississippi Delta Hip-Hop Story
(2009) Let the World Listen Right: The Mississippi Delta Hip-Hop Story, pp. 1-219.
PUBLISHER: University Press of Mississippi
LANGUAGE OF ORIGINAL DOCUMENT: English
DOCUMENT TYPE: Book

Ismer, S.
The search for style and the urge for fame: Emotion regulation and hip-hop culture
(2009) Emotions as Bio-cultural Processes, pp. 351-370.
PUBLISHER: Springer US
LANGUAGE OF ORIGINAL DOCUMENT: English
DOCUMENT TYPE: Book Chapter

Harrison, A.K.
Multiracial youth scenes and the dynamics of race: New approaches to racialization within the bay area hip hop underground
(2009) Twenty-First Century Color Lines: Multiracial Change in Contemporary America, pp. 201-219.
PUBLISHER: Temple University Press
LANGUAGE OF ORIGINAL DOCUMENT: English
DOCUMENT TYPE: Book Chapter

Schur, R.L.
Parodies of ownership: Hip-hop aesthetics and intellectual

property law
(2009) Parodies of Ownership: Hip-Hop Aesthetics and Intellectual Property Law, pp. 1-236.
PUBLISHER: University of Michigan Press
LANGUAGE OF ORIGINAL DOCUMENT: English
DOCUMENT TYPE: Book

Ventura, T.
Hip-hop and graffiti in Rio de Janeiro and São Paulo: A comparative approach [Hip-hop e graffiti: Uma abordagem comparativa entre o Rio de Janeiro e São Paulo]
(2009) Analise Social, 44 (192), pp. 605-634.
LANGUAGE OF ORIGINAL DOCUMENT: Portuguese
DOCUMENT TYPE: Article

Lee, J.
Open mic: Professionalizing the rap career
(2009) Ethnography, 10 (4), pp. 475-495.
LANGUAGE OF ORIGINAL DOCUMENT: English
DOCUMENT TYPE: Article

Antoszek, A.
"the higher the satellite, the lower the culture"? African American studies in East-Central and Southeastern Europe: The case of Poland
(2009) Journal of Transnational American Studies, 1 (1), .
LANGUAGE OF ORIGINAL DOCUMENT: English
DOCUMENT TYPE: Article

Tinsley, B., Wilson, S., Spencer, M.B.
Commentary: Hip-hop culture, youth creativity, and the generational crossroads from a human development perspective
(2009) Art and Human Development, pp. 83-97.
PUBLISHER: Psychology Press Taylor & Francis Group
LANGUAGE OF ORIGINAL DOCUMENT: English
DOCUMENT TYPE: Note

Forman, M.
Hip-hop culture, youth creativity, and the generational crossroads

(2009) Art and Human Development, pp. 59-81.
PUBLISHER: Psychology Press Taylor & Francis Group
LANGUAGE OF ORIGINAL DOCUMENT: English
DOCUMENT TYPE: Book Chapter

Graves, S.
Hip hop: A postmodern folk music
(2009) Sound, Society and the Geography of Popular Music, pp. 245-260.
PUBLISHER: Ashgate Publishing Ltd
LANGUAGE OF ORIGINAL DOCUMENT: English
DOCUMENT TYPE: Book Chapter

Perry, M.D.
Hip hop's diasporic landscapes of blackness
(2009) From Toussaint to Tupac: The Black International since the Age of Revolution, pp. 232-258.
PUBLISHER: The University of North Carolina Press
LANGUAGE OF ORIGINAL DOCUMENT: English
DOCUMENT TYPE: Book Chapter

Cathcart, A.
North Korean hip hop? Reflections on musical diplomacy and the DPRK
(2009) Acta Koreana, 12 (2), pp. 1-19.
LANGUAGE OF ORIGINAL DOCUMENT: English
DOCUMENT TYPE: Article

Anderson, T.L., Kavanaugh, P.R., Rapp, L., Daly, K.
Variations in clubbers' substance use by individual and scene-level factors [Variaciones en el uso de substancias entre clubbers de acuerdo con factores individuales y de nivel de escena]
(2009) Adicciones, 21 (4), pp. 289-308.
LANGUAGE OF ORIGINAL DOCUMENT: Spanish; English
DOCUMENT TYPE: Article

Zhu, Y., Manders, C.M., Farbiz, F., Rahardja, S.
Music feature analysis for synchronization with dance animation

(2009) IEEE Region 10 Annual International Conference,

Proceedings/TENCON, art. no. 5396035, .
CONFERENCE NAME: 2009 IEEE Region 10 Conference, TENCON 2009
CONFERENCE DATE: 23 November 2009 through 26 November 2009
CONFERENCE LOCATION: Singapore
LANGUAGE OF ORIGINAL DOCUMENT: English
DOCUMENT TYPE: Conference Paper

De Gregorio, F., Sung, Y.
Giving a shout out to Seagram's gin: Extent of and attitudes towards brands in popular songs
(2009) Journal of Brand Management, 17 (3), pp. 218-235.
LANGUAGE OF ORIGINAL DOCUMENT: English
DOCUMENT TYPE: Article

Tan, H.L., Zhu, Y., Chaisorn, L., Huang, H.
Sequential rhythmic information retrieval for audio similarity matching
(2009) IEEE Region 10 Annual International Conference, Proceedings/TENCON, art. no. 5396033, .
CONFERENCE NAME: 2009 IEEE Region 10 Conference, TENCON 2009

CONFERENCE DATE: 23 November 2009 through 26 November 2009
CONFERENCE LOCATION: Singapore
LANGUAGE OF ORIGINAL DOCUMENT: English
DOCUMENT TYPE: Conference Paper

Chen, S.-H., Chen, S.-H.
Content-based music genre classification using timbral feature vectors and support vector machine
(2009) ACM International Conference Proceeding Series, 403, pp. 1095-1101.
SPONSORS: ETRI; KISTI; AICIT
CONFERENCE NAME: 2nd International Conference on Interaction Sciences: Information Technology, Culture and Human, ICIS 2009
CONFERENCE DATE: 24 November 2009 through 26 November 2009
CONFERENCE LOCATION: Seoul
LANGUAGE OF ORIGINAL DOCUMENT: English
DOCUMENT TYPE: Conference Paper

Pieslak, J.
Sound targets: American soldiers and music in the Iraq war
(2009) Sound Targets: American Soldiers and Music in the Iraq War, pp. 1-226.
PUBLISHER: Indiana University Press
LANGUAGE OF ORIGINAL DOCUMENT: English
DOCUMENT TYPE: Book

Drissel, D.
Reinventing rebellion: Alternative youth subcultures in Post-Tiananmen China
(2009) International Journal of Interdisciplinary Social Sciences, 3 (10), pp. 39-59.
LANGUAGE OF ORIGINAL DOCUMENT: English
DOCUMENT TYPE: Article

Prestholdt, J.
The afterlives of 2Pac: Imagery and alienation in Sierra Leone and beyond

(2009) Journal of African Cultural Studies, 21 (2), pp. 197-218.
LANGUAGE OF ORIGINAL DOCUMENT: English
DOCUMENT TYPE: Review

Jeger, F., Lussi, A., Zimmerli, B.
Oral jewelry: a review [Schmuck im Mundbereich: eine Ubersicht.]
(2009) Schweizer Monatsschrift für Zahnmedizin = Revue mensuelle suisse d'odonto-stomatologie = Rivista mensile svizzera di odontologia e stomatologia / SSO, 119 (6), pp. 615-631.
LANGUAGE OF ORIGINAL DOCUMENT: German
DOCUMENT TYPE: Review

Germana, M.
Standards of value: Money, race, and literature in America
(2009) Standards of Value: Money, Race, and Literature in America, pp. 1-190.
PUBLISHER: University of Iowa Press
LANGUAGE OF ORIGINAL DOCUMENT: English
DOCUMENT TYPE: Book

Natapoff, A.
Snitching: Criminal informants and the erosion of American justice
(2009) Snitching: Criminal Informants and the Erosion of American Justice, pp. 1-260.
PUBLISHER: New York University Press
LANGUAGE OF ORIGINAL DOCUMENT: English
DOCUMENT TYPE: Book

Aslinger, B.
Genre in genre: The role of music in music games
(2009) Breaking New Ground: Innovation in Games, Play, Practice and Theory - Proceedings of DiGRA 2009, 8 p.
CONFERENCE NAME: 4th Digital Games Research Association International Conference: Breaking New Ground: Innovation in Games, Play, Practice and Theory, DiGRA 2009
CONFERENCE DATE: 1 September 2009 through 4 September 2009
CONFERENCE LOCATION: London

LANGUAGE OF ORIGINAL DOCUMENT: English
DOCUMENT TYPE: Conference Paper

Bloom, P.J.
The state of French cultural exceptionalism: The 2005 uprisings and the politics of visibility
(2009) Frenchness and The African Diaspora: Identity and Uprising in Contemporary France, pp. 227-247.
PUBLISHER: Indiana University Press
LANGUAGE OF ORIGINAL DOCUMENT: English
DOCUMENT TYPE: Book Chapter

Rizzo, M.
"For us, by Us": Hip-hop fashion, commodity blackness and the culture of emulation
(2009) Testimonial Advertising in the American Marketplace: Emulation, Identity, Community, pp. 207-230.
PUBLISHER: Palgrave Macmillan
LANGUAGE OF ORIGINAL DOCUMENT: English
DOCUMENT TYPE: Book Chapter

Abe, D.
Hip-hop and the academic canon
(2009) Education, Citizenship and Social Justice, 4 (3), pp. 263-272.
LANGUAGE OF ORIGINAL DOCUMENT: English
DOCUMENT TYPE: Article

Pfadenhauer, M.
The lord of the loops. Observations at the club culture DJ-desk
(2009) Forum Qualitative Sozialforschung, 10 (3), .
LANGUAGE OF ORIGINAL DOCUMENT: English
DOCUMENT TYPE: Article

Roy, A.G.
Punjabi delights in forbidden city Singapore: The space of flows and place
(2009) Sojourn, 24 (2), pp. 236-250.

LANGUAGE OF ORIGINAL DOCUMENT: English
DOCUMENT TYPE: Article

Anderson, T., Daly, K., Rapp, L.
Clubbing masculinities and crime: A qualitative study of Philadelphia nightclub scenes
(2009) Feminist Criminology, 4 (4), pp. 302-332.
LANGUAGE OF ORIGINAL DOCUMENT: English
DOCUMENT TYPE: Article

Clarke, S., Hiscock, P.
Hip-hop in a Post-insular community: Hybridity, local language, and authenticity in an online Newfoundland rap group
(2009) Journal of English Linguistics, 37 (3), pp. 241-261.
LANGUAGE OF ORIGINAL DOCUMENT: English
DOCUMENT TYPE: Article

Greenberg, E.
'The king of the streets': Hip hop and the reclaiming of masculinity in Jerusalem's Shu'afat Refugee Camp
(2009) Middle East Journal of Culture and Communication, 2 (2), pp. 231-250.
LANGUAGE OF ORIGINAL DOCUMENT: English

DOCUMENT TYPE: Review

Fletcher, H.
Finding success at the source : Co-owner and executive publisher L. Londell McMillan reveals how he plans to revive the ailing hip-hop brand in a difficult economy
(2009) Publishing Executive, 24 (7), pp. 14-15.
LANGUAGE OF ORIGINAL DOCUMENT: English
DOCUMENT TYPE: Article

García-Romero, A.
Fugue, hip hop and soap opera: Transcultural connections and theatrical experimentation in twenty-first century US Latina playwriting
(2009) Latin American Theatre Review, 43 (1), pp. 87-102.
LANGUAGE OF ORIGINAL DOCUMENT: English
DOCUMENT TYPE: Review

Kish, Z.
"My FEMA people": Hip-hop as disaster recovery in the Katrina Diaspora
(2009) American Quarterly, 61 (3), pp. 671-692.
LANGUAGE OF ORIGINAL DOCUMENT: English
DOCUMENT TYPE: Review

Solomon, T.
Berlin-Frankfurt-Istanbul: Turkish hip-hop in motion
(2009) European Journal of Cultural Studies, 12 (3), pp. 305-327.
LANGUAGE OF ORIGINAL DOCUMENT: English
DOCUMENT TYPE: Article

Kajikawa, L.
Eminem's "My Name Is": Signifying whiteness, Rearticulating race
(2009) Journal of the Society for American Music, 3 (3), pp. 341-363.
LANGUAGE OF ORIGINAL DOCUMENT: English
DOCUMENT TYPE: Article

Podkalicka, A.
Young listening: An ethnography of YouthWorx Media's radio project
(2009) Continuum, 23 (4), pp. 561-572.
LANGUAGE OF ORIGINAL DOCUMENT: English
DOCUMENT TYPE: Review

Hammett, D.
Local beats to global rhythms: Coloured student identity and negotiations of global cultural imports in Cape Town, South Africa
(2009) Social and Cultural Geography, 10 (4), pp. 403-419.
LANGUAGE OF ORIGINAL DOCUMENT: English
DOCUMENT TYPE: Article

A hip-hop happening they had of it
(2009) Economist, 392 (8638), .
LANGUAGE OF ORIGINAL DOCUMENT: English
DOCUMENT TYPE: Short Survey

Hill, M.L.
Bringing back sweet (and not so sweet) memories: The cultural politics of memory, hip-hop, and generational identities
(2009) International Journal of Qualitative Studies in Education, 22 (4), pp. 355-377.
LANGUAGE OF ORIGINAL DOCUMENT: English
DOCUMENT TYPE: Article

Petchauer, E.
Framing and reviewing hip-hop educational research
(2009) Review of Educational Research, 79 (2), pp. 946-978.
LANGUAGE OF ORIGINAL DOCUMENT: English
DOCUMENT TYPE: Review

Shipley, J.W.
Aesthetic of the entrepreneur: Afro-cosmopolitan rap and moral circulation in Accra, Ghana
(2009) Anthropological Quarterly, 82 (3), pp. 631-668.

LANGUAGE OF ORIGINAL DOCUMENT: English
DOCUMENT TYPE: Article

Pedersen, W.
Cannabis use: Subcultural opposition or social marginality?: A population-based longitudinal study
(2009) Acta Sociologica, 52 (2), pp. 135-148.
LANGUAGE OF ORIGINAL DOCUMENT: English
DOCUMENT TYPE: Article

Devane, B.
'Get some secured credit cards homey': Hip hop discourse, financial literacy and the design of digital media learning environments
(2009) E-Learning, 6 (1), pp. 4-22.
PUBLISHER: Symposium Journals
LANGUAGE OF ORIGINAL DOCUMENT: English
DOCUMENT TYPE: Article

McCorkel, J., Rodriquez, J.
"Are you an African?" The politics of self-construction in status-based social movements
(2009) Social Problems, 56 (2), pp. 357-384.
PUBLISHER: University of California Press
LANGUAGE OF ORIGINAL DOCUMENT: English
DOCUMENT TYPE: Article

Reyna, C., Brandt, M., Tendayi Viki, G.
Blame it on hip-hop: Anti-rap attitudes as a proxy for prejudice
(2009) Group Processes and Intergroup Relations, 12 (3), pp. 361-380.
PUBLISHER: SAGE Publications Ltd
LANGUAGE OF ORIGINAL DOCUMENT: English
DOCUMENT TYPE: Article

Irizarry, J.G.
Representin' Drawing from hip-hop and Urban youth culture to inform teacher education
(2009) Education and Urban Society, 41 (4), pp. 489-515.

LANGUAGE OF ORIGINAL DOCUMENT: English
DOCUMENT TYPE: Article

Tavares, B.L.

In the slope, the partnership is stronger - A youth hip-hop: Relationship and strategies against the discrimination in the periphery of the Federal area [Na quebrada, a parceria é mais forte - Juventude hip-hop: Relacionamento e estratégias contra a discriminação na periferia do distrito federal]
(2009) Sociedade e Estado, 24 (2), p. 615.
LANGUAGE OF ORIGINAL DOCUMENT: Portuguese
DOCUMENT TYPE: Article

Oware, M.

A man's woman? Contradictory messages in the songs of female rappers, 1992-2000
(2009) Journal of Black Studies, 39 (5), pp. 786-802.
LANGUAGE OF ORIGINAL DOCUMENT: English
DOCUMENT TYPE: Article

Tjora, A.H.
The groove in the box: A technologically mediated inspiration in electronic dance music

(2009) Popular Music, 28 (2), pp. 161-177.
LANGUAGE OF ORIGINAL DOCUMENT: English
DOCUMENT TYPE: Review

Chang, V.
Records that play: The present past in sampling practice
(2009) Popular Music, 28 (2), pp. 143-159.
LANGUAGE OF ORIGINAL DOCUMENT: English
DOCUMENT TYPE: Review

Baker, L.D.
Saggin' and Braggin'
(2009) Anthropology off the Shelf: Anthropologists on Writing, pp. 46-59.
PUBLISHER: Wiley-Blackwell
LANGUAGE OF ORIGINAL DOCUMENT: English
DOCUMENT TYPE: Book Chapter

Emdin, C.
Reality pedagogy: Hip hop culture and the urban science classroom
(2009) Science Education from People for People: Taking a Stand(point), pp. 70-89.
PUBLISHER: Routledge Taylor & Francis Group
LANGUAGE OF ORIGINAL DOCUMENT: English
DOCUMENT TYPE: Book Chapter

Gonzalez, T., Hayes, B.G.
Rap music in school counseling based on don Elligan's rap therapy
(2009) Journal of Creativity in Mental Health, 4 (2), pp. 161-172.
LANGUAGE OF ORIGINAL DOCUMENT: English
DOCUMENT TYPE: Article

El-Khairy, O.
'Freedom's a lifestyle choice': US cultural diplomacy, empire's soundtrack, and middle eastern 'youth' in our contemporary global infowar

(2009) Middle East Journal of Culture and Communication, 2 (1), pp. 115-135.
LANGUAGE OF ORIGINAL DOCUMENT: English
DOCUMENT TYPE: Review

Yim, J.-D., Shaw, C.D., Bartram, L.
Musician Map: Visualizing music collaborations over time
(2009) Proceedings of SPIE - The International Society for Optical Engineering, 7243, art. no. 72430A, .
CONFERENCE NAME: Visualization and Data Analysis 2009
CONFERENCE DATE: 19 January 2009 through 20 January 2009
CONFERENCE LOCATION: San Jose, CA
LANGUAGE OF ORIGINAL DOCUMENT: English
DOCUMENT TYPE: Conference Paper

Pritchard, G.
Cultural imperialism, Americanisation and Cape Town hip-hop culture: A discussion piece
(2009) Social Dynamics, 35 (1), pp. 51-55.
LANGUAGE OF ORIGINAL DOCUMENT: English
DOCUMENT TYPE: Article

Ball, J.
FreeMix radio: The original mixtape radio show: A case study in mixtape "radio" and emancipatory journalism
(2009) Journal of Black Studies, 39 (4), pp. 614-634.
LANGUAGE OF ORIGINAL DOCUMENT: English
DOCUMENT TYPE: Article

Omoniyi, T., Scheid, S., Oni, D.
Negotiating youth identity in a transnational context in Nigeria
(2009) Social Dynamics, 35 (1), pp. 1-18.
LANGUAGE OF ORIGINAL DOCUMENT: English
DOCUMENT TYPE: Article

Mulder, J., Ter Bogt, T.F.M., Raaijmakers, Q.A.W., Gabhainn, S.N., Monshouwer, K., Vollebergh, W.A.M.
The soundtrack of substance use: Music preference and

adolescent smoking and drinking
(2009) Substance Use and Misuse, 44 (4), pp. 514-531.
LANGUAGE OF ORIGINAL DOCUMENT: English
DOCUMENT TYPE: Article

Rodriguez, L.F.
Dialoguing, cultural capital, and student engagement: Toward a hip hop pedagogy in the high school and university classroom
(2009) Equity and Excellence in Education, 42 (1), pp. 20-35.
LANGUAGE OF ORIGINAL DOCUMENT: English
DOCUMENT TYPE: Article

Hallman, H.L.
"Dear Tupac, you speak to me": Recruiting hip hop as curriculum at a School for Pregnant and Parenting Teens
(2009) Equity and Excellence in Education, 42 (1), pp. 36-51.
LANGUAGE OF ORIGINAL DOCUMENT: English
DOCUMENT TYPE: Article

Baszile, D.T.
Deal with it we must: Education, social justice, and the curriculum of hip hop culture
(2009) Equity and Excellence in Education, 42 (1), pp. 6-19.
LANGUAGE OF ORIGINAL DOCUMENT: English
DOCUMENT TYPE: Article

Pulido, I.
"Music fit for us minorities": Latinas/os' use of hip hop as pedagogy and interpretive framework to negotiate and challenge racism
(2009) Equity and Excellence in Education, 42 (1), pp. 67-85.
LANGUAGE OF ORIGINAL DOCUMENT: English
DOCUMENT TYPE: Article

Akom, A.A.
Critical hip hop pedagogy as a form of liberatory praxis
(2009) Equity and Excellence in Education, 42 (1), pp. 52-66.
LANGUAGE OF ORIGINAL DOCUMENT: English

DOCUMENT TYPE: Article

Hall, M.R.
Hip-hop education resources

(2009) Equity and Excellence in Education, 42 (1), pp. 86-94.
LANGUAGE OF ORIGINAL DOCUMENT: English
DOCUMENT TYPE: Article

Land, R.R., Stovall, D.
Hip hop and Social justice education: A brief introduction
(2009) Equity and Excellence in Education, 42 (1), pp. 1-5.
LANGUAGE OF ORIGINAL DOCUMENT: English
DOCUMENT TYPE: Editorial

Hill, M.L.
Scared straight: Hip-Hop, outing, and the pedagogy of queerness
(2009) Review of Education, Pedagogy, and Cultural Studies, 31 (1), pp.
29-54.
LANGUAGE OF ORIGINAL DOCUMENT: English
DOCUMENT TYPE: Article

Low, B., Sarkar, M., Winer, L.

'Ch'us mon propre Bescherelle': Challenges from the Hip-Hop nation to the Quebec nation
(2009) Journal of Sociolinguistics, 13 (1), pp. 59-82.
LANGUAGE OF ORIGINAL DOCUMENT: English
DOCUMENT TYPE: Article
ACCESS TYPE: Open Access

Kuppens, A.H.
Authenticating subcultural identities: African American and Jamaican English in niche media
(2009) Journal of Communication Inquiry, 33 (1), pp. 43-57.
LANGUAGE OF ORIGINAL DOCUMENT: English
DOCUMENT TYPE: Article

Wright, R.R., Sandlin, J.A.
Cult TV, hip hop, shape-shifters, and vampire slayers: A review of the literature at the intersection of adult education and popular culture
(2009) Adult Education Quarterly, 59 (2), pp. 118-141.
LANGUAGE OF ORIGINAL DOCUMENT: English
DOCUMENT TYPE: Article

Alim, H.S.
Translocal style communities: Hip Hop youth as cultural theorists of style, language, and globalization
(2009) Pragmatics, 19 (1), pp. 103-127.
PUBLISHER: International Pragmatics Association
LANGUAGE OF ORIGINAL DOCUMENT: English
DOCUMENT TYPE: Article

Khan, K.
Chinese hip hop music: Negotiating for cultural freedoms in the 21st century
(2009) Muziki, 6 (2), pp. 232-240.
LANGUAGE OF ORIGINAL DOCUMENT: English
DOCUMENT TYPE: Article

Fraley, T.

I got a natural skill: Hip-hop, authenticity, and whiteness
(2009) Howard Journal of Communications, 20 (1), pp. 37-54.
LANGUAGE OF ORIGINAL DOCUMENT: English
DOCUMENT TYPE: Article

Moreno, R.C., Almeida, A.M.F.
Young people's political engagement in the hip-hop movement [O engajamento político dos jovens no movimento hip-hop]
(2009) Revista Brasileira de Educacao, 14 (40), pp. 130-142.
LANGUAGE OF ORIGINAL DOCUMENT: Portuguese
DOCUMENT TYPE: Article
ACCESS TYPE: Open Access

Harrison, A.K.
Hip hop underground: The integrity and ethics of racial identification
(2009) Hip Hop Underground: The Integrity and Ethics of Racial Identification, 9781439900628, pp. 1-219.
PUBLISHER: Temple University Press
LANGUAGE OF ORIGINAL DOCUMENT: English
DOCUMENT TYPE: Book

Thompson, K.
The sound of light: Reflections on art history in the visual culture of hip-hop
(2009) Art Bulletin, 91 (4), pp. 481-505.
PUBLISHER: College Art Association
LANGUAGE OF ORIGINAL DOCUMENT: English
DOCUMENT TYPE: Article

Hill, M.L.
Wounded healing: Forming a storytelling community in hip-hop lit
(2009) Teachers College Record, 111 (1), pp. 248-293.
PUBLISHER: Teachers College, Columbia University
LANGUAGE OF ORIGINAL DOCUMENT: English
DOCUMENT TYPE: Article

Thomas, G.
Hip-hop revolution in the flesh: Power, knowledge, and pleasure in Lil' Kim's lyricism
(2009) Hip-Hop Revolution in the Flesh: Power, Knowledge, and Pleasure in Lil' Kim's Lyricism, pp. 1-231.
PUBLISHER: Palgrave Macmillan
LANGUAGE OF ORIGINAL DOCUMENT: English
DOCUMENT TYPE: Book

Cohen, J.
Hip-hop Judaica: The politics of representin' Heebster heritage
(2009) Popular Music, 28 (1), pp. 1-18.
LANGUAGE OF ORIGINAL DOCUMENT: English
DOCUMENT TYPE: Review

Quested, E., Duda, J.L.
Perceptions of the motivational climate, need satisfaction, and indices of well- and ill-being among hip hop dancers.
(2009) Journal of dance medicine & science : official publication of the International Association for Dance Medicine & Science, 13 (1), pp. 10-19.
LANGUAGE OF ORIGINAL DOCUMENT: English
DOCUMENT TYPE: Article

Casamayor-Cisneros, O.
Confrontation and occurrence: Ethical–esthetic expressions of blackness in post-soviet cuba
(2009) Latin American and Caribbean Ethnic Studies, 4 (2), pp. 103-135.
LANGUAGE OF ORIGINAL DOCUMENT: English
DOCUMENT TYPE: Article

Daniel, O.
Virtual primordialism: Transnational networks and cultural production of diaspora [Virtuální primordialismus: Transnacionální sítě a kulturní produkce diaspory (příklady Bosňáků a Kabylů)]
(2009) Socialni Studia, 6 (1), pp. 113-126.
PUBLISHER: Masaryk University
LANGUAGE OF ORIGINAL DOCUMENT: Czech
DOCUMENT TYPE: Article

Stephens, D.P., Phillips, L.D., Few, A.L.
Examining African American female adolescent sexuality within mainstream hip hop culture using a womanist-ecological model of human development

(2009) Handbook of Feminist Family Studies, pp. 160-173.
PUBLISHER: SAGE Publications Inc.
LANGUAGE OF ORIGINAL DOCUMENT: English
DOCUMENT TYPE: Book Chapter

Yasin, J.A.
Hip hop: A source of empowerment for African American male college students
(2009) The SAGE Handbook of African American Education, pp. 283-296.
PUBLISHER: SAGE Publications Inc.
LANGUAGE OF ORIGINAL DOCUMENT: English

DOCUMENT TYPE: Book Chapter

Hayes, B.
Hip-hop physics
(2009) American Scientist, 97 (6), pp. 438-442.
PUBLISHER: Sigma Xi, Scientific Research Society
LANGUAGE OF ORIGINAL DOCUMENT: English
DOCUMENT TYPE: Article

Chari, T.
Continuity and change: Impact of global popular culture on urban grooves music in Zimbabwe
(2009) Muziki, 6 (2), pp. 170-191.
LANGUAGE OF ORIGINAL DOCUMENT: English
DOCUMENT TYPE: Article

Jones, S.H.
The textbattle and the contention of youth identities online: An ethnographic case study
(2009) German Life and Letters, 62 (1), pp. 96-113.
LANGUAGE OF ORIGINAL DOCUMENT: English
DOCUMENT TYPE: Review

Higgins, C.
English as a local language: Post-colonial identities and multilingual practices
(2009) English as a Local Language: Post-Colonial Identities and Multilingual Practices, pp. 1-171.
PUBLISHER: Channel View Publications
LANGUAGE OF ORIGINAL DOCUMENT: English
DOCUMENT TYPE: Book

Beaulac, J., Bouchard, D., Kristjansson, E.
Physical activity for adolescents living in a disadvantaged neighbourhood: Views of parents and adolescents on needs, barriers, facilitators, and programming
(2009) Leisure/ Loisir, 33 (2), pp. 537-561.
LANGUAGE OF ORIGINAL DOCUMENT: English

DOCUMENT TYPE: Article

Sandberg, S., Pedersen, W.
Street capital: Black cannabis dealers in a white welfare state
(2009) Street Capital: Black Cannabis Dealers in a White Welfare State, pp. 1-194.
  PUBLISHER: Policy Press
  LANGUAGE OF ORIGINAL DOCUMENT: English
  DOCUMENT TYPE: Book

Grandt, J.E.
Shaping Words to Fit the Soul: The Southern Ritual Grounds of Afro-Modernism
(2009) Shaping Words to Fit the Soul: The Southern Ritual Grounds of Afro-Modernism, pp. 1-192.
  PUBLISHER: Ohio State University Press
  LANGUAGE OF ORIGINAL DOCUMENT: English
  DOCUMENT TYPE: Book

West, M.O., Martin, W.G., Wilkins, F.C.
From toussaint to tupac: The black international since the age of revolution
(2009) From Toussaint to Tupac: The Black International since the Age of Revolution, pp. 1-318.
  PUBLISHER: University of North Carolina Press
  LANGUAGE OF ORIGINAL DOCUMENT: English
  DOCUMENT TYPE: Book

Leach, A.
One day it'll all make sense: Hip-hop and rap resources for music librarians
(2008) Notes, 65 (1), pp. 9-37.
  LANGUAGE OF ORIGINAL DOCUMENT: English
  DOCUMENT TYPE: Review

Greenwald, J.
Hip-hop drumming: The rhyme may define, but the groove makes you move

(2008) Black Music Research Journal, 22 (2), pp. 259-271.
LANGUAGE OF ORIGINAL DOCUMENT: English
DOCUMENT TYPE: Article

Caramanica, J.
Hip-hop heirlooms
(2008) Architectural Digest, 65 (9 SUPPL), .
LANGUAGE OF ORIGINAL DOCUMENT: English
DOCUMENT TYPE: Note

Shankar, S.
Speaking like a model minority: "FOB" styles, gender, and racial meanings among desi teens in Silicon Valley
(2008) Journal of Linguistic Anthropology, 18 (2), pp. 268-289.
LANGUAGE OF ORIGINAL DOCUMENT: English
DOCUMENT TYPE: Article

Perry, M.D.
Global black self-fashionings: Hip hop as diasporic space
(2008) Identities, 15 (6), pp. 635-664.
LANGUAGE OF ORIGINAL DOCUMENT: English
DOCUMENT TYPE: Article

Knobloch-Westerwick, S., Musto, P., Shaw, K.
Rebellion in the Top Music Charts: Defiant Messages in Rap/Hip-Hop and Rock Music 1993 and 2003
(2008) Journal of Media Psychology, 20 (1), pp. 15-23.
LANGUAGE OF ORIGINAL DOCUMENT: English
DOCUMENT TYPE: Article

Swartz, S.
Is Kwaito South African hip-hop? Why the answer matters and who it matters to
(2008) World of Music, 50 (2), pp. 15-33.
LANGUAGE OF ORIGINAL DOCUMENT: English
DOCUMENT TYPE: Article

Turner-Musa, J.O., Rhodes, W.A., Harper, P.T.H., Quinton, S.L.
Hip-hop to prevent substance use and HIV among African-American youth: A preliminary investigation
(2008) Journal of Drug Education, 38 (4), pp. 351-365.
LANGUAGE OF ORIGINAL DOCUMENT: English

DOCUMENT TYPE: Article

Pardue, D.

Performing attitude: An imposing space and gender by Brazilian hip hoppers [Desempenhando atitude: Uma imposição de espaço e gênero pelos hip hoppers Brasileiros]
(2008) Revista de Antropologia, 51 (2), pp. 519-546.
LANGUAGE OF ORIGINAL DOCUMENT: English; Portuguese
DOCUMENT TYPE: Article

Devitt, R.
Lost in translation: Filipino diaspora(s), postcolonial hip hop, and the problems of keeping it real for the "contentless" Black Eyed Peas
(2008) Asian Music, 39 (1), pp. 108-134.
LANGUAGE OF ORIGINAL DOCUMENT: English
DOCUMENT TYPE: Review

Fung, A.
Western style, Chinese pop: Jay Chou's rap and hip-hop in China
(2008) Asian Music, 39 (1), pp. 69-80.
LANGUAGE OF ORIGINAL DOCUMENT: English
DOCUMENT TYPE: Review

McFarland, P.
Chicano rap: Gender and violence in the postindustrial barrio
(2008) Chicano Rap: Gender and Violence in the Postindustrial Barrio, pp. 1-198.
PUBLISHER: University of Texas Press
LANGUAGE OF ORIGINAL DOCUMENT: English
DOCUMENT TYPE: Book

Mattar, Y.
Miso soup for the ears: Contemporary Japanese popular music and its relation to the genres familiar to the anglophonic audience
(2008) Popular Music and Society, 31 (1), pp. 113-123.
LANGUAGE OF ORIGINAL DOCUMENT: English
DOCUMENT TYPE: Review

Chalmers, T.D., Arthur, D.
Hard-core members' of consumption-oriented subcultures enactment of identity: The sacred consumption of two subcultures

(2008) Advances in Consumer Research, 35, pp. 570-575.
LANGUAGE OF ORIGINAL DOCUMENT: English
DOCUMENT TYPE: Conference Paper

Shuker, R.
New Zealand popular music, government policy, and cultural identity
(2008) Popular Music, 27 (2), pp. 271-287.
LANGUAGE OF ORIGINAL DOCUMENT: English
DOCUMENT TYPE: Review

Stratton, J.
The Beastie Boys: Jews in whiteface
(2008) Popular Music, 27 (3), pp. 413-432.
LANGUAGE OF ORIGINAL DOCUMENT: English
DOCUMENT TYPE: Review

Morrison, A.M.
Musical trafficking: Urban youth and the narcocorrido-hardcore rap nexus
(2008) Western Folklore, 67 (4), pp. 379-396.
LANGUAGE OF ORIGINAL DOCUMENT: English
DOCUMENT TYPE: Article

Dreisinger, B.
Near black: White-to-black passing in American culture
(2008) Near Black: White-to-Black Passing in American Culture, pp. 1-184.
PUBLISHER: University of Massachusetts Press
LANGUAGE OF ORIGINAL DOCUMENT: English
DOCUMENT TYPE: Book

Hughey, M.W.
Cuz i'm young and i'm black and my hat's real low?: A critique of black greeks as "educated gangs"
(2008) Black Greek-letter Organizations in the Twenty-First Century, pp. 385-418.
PUBLISHER: The University Press of Kentucky

LANGUAGE OF ORIGINAL DOCUMENT: English
DOCUMENT TYPE: Book Chapter

Capino, J.B.
1997: Movies and the usable past
(2008) American Cinema of The 1990s: Themes and Variations, pp. 180-202.
PUBLISHER: Rutgers University Press
LANGUAGE OF ORIGINAL DOCUMENT: English
DOCUMENT TYPE: Book Chapter

Willis, S.
1991: Movies and wayward images
(2008) American Cinema of The 1990s: Themes and Variations, pp. 45-69.
PUBLISHER: Rutgers University Press
LANGUAGE OF ORIGINAL DOCUMENT: English
DOCUMENT TYPE: Book Chapter

Danielsen, A.
The musicalization of 'reality': Reality rap and rap reality on Public Enemy's Fear of a Black Planet
(2008) European Journal of Cultural Studies, 11 (4), pp. 405-421.
LANGUAGE OF ORIGINAL DOCUMENT: English
DOCUMENT TYPE: Article

Akom, A.A.
Black metropolis and mental life: Beyond the "burden of 'acting white'" toward a third wave of critical racial studies
(2008) Anthropology and Education Quarterly, 39 (3), pp. 247-265.
LANGUAGE OF ORIGINAL DOCUMENT: English
DOCUMENT TYPE: Article

Geller, J.
A mixtape DJ's Drama: An argument for copyright preemption of Georgia's unauthorized reproduction law
(2008) Journal of Intellectual Property, 8 (1), .
LANGUAGE OF ORIGINAL DOCUMENT: English

DOCUMENT TYPE: Article

Williams, O., Noble, J.M.
'Hip-Hop' stroke: A stroke educational program for elementary school children living in a high-risk community
(2008) Stroke, 39 (10), pp. 2809-2816.
LANGUAGE OF ORIGINAL DOCUMENT: English
DOCUMENT TYPE: Article
ACCESS TYPE: Open Access

Matsunaga, P.S.
Woman's social representations in the hip-hop movement [As representações sociais da mulher no movimento hip hop]
(2008) Psicologia e Sociedade, 20 (1), pp. 108-116.
LANGUAGE OF ORIGINAL DOCUMENT: Portuguese
DOCUMENT TYPE: Article

Tickner, A.B.
Aquíen el Ghetto: Hip-hop in Colombia, Cuba, and Mexico
(2008) Latin American Politics and Society, 50 (3), pp. 121-146.
LANGUAGE OF ORIGINAL DOCUMENT: English
DOCUMENT TYPE: Article

Alim, H.S., Ibrahim, A., Pennycook, A.
Global linguistic flows: Hip hop cultures, youth identities, and the politics of language
(2008) Global Linguistic Flows: Hip Hop Cultures, Youth Identities, and the Politics of Language, pp. 1-260.
PUBLISHER: Routledge Taylor & Francis Group
LANGUAGE OF ORIGINAL DOCUMENT: English
DOCUMENT TYPE: Book

Androutsopoulos, J.
Language and the three spheres of Hip Hop
(2008) Global Linguistic Flows: Hip Hop Cultures, Youth Identities, and the Politics of Language, pp. 43-62.
PUBLISHER: Routledge Taylor & Francis Group
LANGUAGE OF ORIGINAL DOCUMENT: English
DOCUMENT TYPE: Book Chapter

Alim, H.S.
Creating "an empire within an empire": Critical Hip Hop language pedagogies and the role of sociolinguistics
(2008) Global Linguistic Flows: Hip Hop Cultures, Youth Identities, and the Politics of Language, pp. 213-230.
PUBLISHER: Routledge Taylor & Francis Group
LANGUAGE OF ORIGINAL DOCUMENT: English
DOCUMENT TYPE: Book Chapter

Alim, H.S.
Intro: Straight outta Compton, straight aus München: Global linguistic flows, identities, and the politics of language in a global Hip Hop nation
(2008) Global Linguistic Flows: Hip Hop Cultures, Youth Identities, and the Politics of Language, pp. 1-22.
PUBLISHER: Routledge Taylor & Francis Group
LANGUAGE OF ORIGINAL DOCUMENT: English
DOCUMENT TYPE: Editorial

Lin, A.

"Respect for Da Chopstick Hip Hop": The politics, poetics, and pedagogy of cantonese verbal art in Hong Kong
(2008) Global Linguistic Flows: Hip Hop Cultures, Youth Identities, and the Politics of Language, pp. 159-177.
PUBLISHER: Routledge Taylor & Francis Group
LANGUAGE OF ORIGINAL DOCUMENT: English
DOCUMENT TYPE: Book Chapter

Ibrahim, A.
Takin Hip Hop to a whole nother level: Métissage, affect, and pedagogy in a global Hip Hop nation
(2008) Global Linguistic Flows: Hip Hop Cultures, Youth Identities, and the Politics of Language, pp. 231-248.
PUBLISHER: Routledge Taylor & Francis Group
LANGUAGE OF ORIGINAL DOCUMENT: English
DOCUMENT TYPE: Book Chapter

Sarkar, M.
"Still reppin' por mi gente": The transformative power of language mixing in Quebec Hip Hop
(2008) Global Linguistic Flows: Hip Hop Cultures, Youth Identities, and the Politics of Language, pp. 139-157.
PUBLISHER: Routledge Taylor & Francis Group
LANGUAGE OF ORIGINAL DOCUMENT: English
DOCUMENT TYPE: Book Chapter

Tsujimura, N., Davis, S.
Dragon ash and the reinterpretation of Hip Hop: On the notion of rhyme in Japanese Hip Hop
(2008) Global Linguistic Flows: Hip Hop Cultures, Youth Identities, and the Politics of Language, pp. 179-193.
PUBLISHER: Routledge Taylor & Francis Group
LANGUAGE OF ORIGINAL DOCUMENT: English
DOCUMENT TYPE: Book Chapter

Higgins, C.
From da bomb to Bomba: Global Hip Hop nation language in Tanzania
(2008) Global Linguistic Flows: Hip Hop Cultures, Youth Identities, and

the Politics of Language, pp. 95-112.
    PUBLISHER: Routledge Taylor & Francis Group
    LANGUAGE OF ORIGINAL DOCUMENT: English
    DOCUMENT TYPE: Book Chapter

Omoniyi, T.
"So I choose to do am Naija style": Hip Hop, language, and postcolonial identities
    (2008) Global Linguistic Flows: Hip Hop Cultures, Youth Identities, and the Politics of Language, pp. 113-135.
    PUBLISHER: Routledge Taylor & Francis Group
    LANGUAGE OF ORIGINAL DOCUMENT: English
    DOCUMENT TYPE: Book Chapter

Roth-Gordon, J.
Conversational sampling, race trafficking, and the invocation of the Gueto in Brazilian Hip Hop
    (2008) Global Linguistic Flows: Hip Hop Cultures, Youth Identities, and the Politics of Language, pp. 63-77.
    PUBLISHER: Routledge Taylor & Francis Group
    LANGUAGE OF ORIGINAL DOCUMENT: English
    DOCUMENT TYPE: Book Chapter

Pennycook, A., Mitchell, T.
Hip Hop as dusty foot philosophy: Engaging locality
    (2008) Global Linguistic Flows: Hip Hop Cultures, Youth Identities, and the Politics of Language, pp. 25-42.
    PUBLISHER: Routledge Taylor & Francis Group
    LANGUAGE OF ORIGINAL DOCUMENT: English
    DOCUMENT TYPE: Book Chapter

Prier, D., Beachum, F.
Conceptualizing a critical discourse around hip-hop culture and Black male youth in educational scholarship and research
    (2008) International Journal of Qualitative Studies in Education, 21 (5), pp. 519-535.
    LANGUAGE OF ORIGINAL DOCUMENT: English
    DOCUMENT TYPE: Article

Maira, S.
"We ain't missing": Palestinian hip hop - A transnational youth movement
(2008) New Centennial Review, 8 (2), pp. 161-192.
LANGUAGE OF ORIGINAL DOCUMENT: English
DOCUMENT TYPE: Review

Hodgson, I.J.
Dust, sugar-cane and hip-hop: Real world research in Africa
(2008) HIV Nursing, 8 (3), pp. 17-20.
LANGUAGE OF ORIGINAL DOCUMENT: English
DOCUMENT TYPE: Article

De Bruijn, E.
"What's love" in an interconnected world? Ghanaian market literature for youth responds
(2008) Journal of Commonwealth Literature, 43 (3), pp. 3-24.
LANGUAGE OF ORIGINAL DOCUMENT: English
DOCUMENT TYPE: Review

Flores, J.
The diaspora strikes back: Caribeño tales of learning and turning
(2008) The Diaspora Strikes Back: Caribeño Tales of Learning and Turning, pp. 1-237.
PUBLISHER: Routledge Taylor & Francis Group
LANGUAGE OF ORIGINAL DOCUMENT: English
DOCUMENT TYPE: Book

Fulmer, R.H.
'Don't save her' - Sigmund Freud meets project Pat: The rescue motif in hip-hop
(2008) International Journal of Psychoanalysis, 89 (4), pp. 727-742.
LANGUAGE OF ORIGINAL DOCUMENT: English
DOCUMENT TYPE: Article

Kroth, J., Lamas, J., Pisca, N., Bourret, K., Kollath, M.
Retrospective dream components and musical preferences
(2008) Psychological Reports, 103 (1), pp. 93-96.
LANGUAGE OF ORIGINAL DOCUMENT: English
DOCUMENT TYPE: Article

Irarrázabal, G.F.
Sobre la estética del graffiti Hip Hop

(2008) Studies in Latin American Popular Culture, 27, pp. 129-149.
LANGUAGE OF ORIGINAL DOCUMENT: Spanish
DOCUMENT TYPE: Article

Reiter, B., Mitchell, G.L.
Embracing hip hop as their own: Hip hop and black racial identity in Brazil
(2008) Studies in Latin American Popular Culture, 27, pp. 151-165.
LANGUAGE OF ORIGINAL DOCUMENT: English
DOCUMENT TYPE: Article

Cox Edmondson, V.
A preliminary review of competitive reactions in the hip-hop music industry: Black American entrepreneurs in a new industry
(2008) Management Research News, 31 (9), pp. 637-649.
LANGUAGE OF ORIGINAL DOCUMENT: English
DOCUMENT TYPE: Article

Distiller, N.
"My People all over the World": Hip Hop, Gender, and Black Nationalism
(2008) Safundi, 9 (3), pp. 351-356.
LANGUAGE OF ORIGINAL DOCUMENT: English
DOCUMENT TYPE: Article

Gropler, M.
Kicking it in the business of selling sneakers for over ten years, snipes is now pushing its street savvy to a new level
(2008) Sportswear International, (220), p. 54.
LANGUAGE OF ORIGINAL DOCUMENT: English
DOCUMENT TYPE: Article

Park, J.S.-Y., Wee, L.
Appropriating the language of the other: Performativity in autonomous and unified markets
(2008) Language and Communication, 28 (3), pp. 242-257.
LANGUAGE OF ORIGINAL DOCUMENT: English
DOCUMENT TYPE: Article

Ceará, A.d.T., Dalgalarrondo, P.
Young graffiter: Psico-social profile. identity and motivation [Jovens pichadores: Perfil psicossocial, identidade e motivação]
(2008) Psicologia USP, 19 (3), pp. 277-293.
LANGUAGE OF ORIGINAL DOCUMENT: Portuguese
DOCUMENT TYPE: Article
ACCESS TYPE: Open Access

The politics of hip-hop
(2008) Economist, 387 (8586), .
LANGUAGE OF ORIGINAL DOCUMENT: English
DOCUMENT TYPE: Article

Selfhout, M.H.W., Delsing, M.J.M.H., Ter Bogt, T.F.M., Meeus, W.H.J.
Heavy metal and hip-hop style preferences and externalizing problem behavior: A two-wave longitudinal study
(2008) Youth and Society, 39 (4), pp. 435-452.
LANGUAGE OF ORIGINAL DOCUMENT: English
DOCUMENT TYPE: Article

Muñoz-Laboy, M.A., Castellanos, D.H., Haliburton, C.S., Del Aguila, E.V., Weinstein, H.J., Parker, R.G.
Condom use and hip hop culture: The case of urban young men in New York City
(2008) American Journal of Public Health, 98 (6), pp. 1081-1085.
LANGUAGE OF ORIGINAL DOCUMENT: English
DOCUMENT TYPE: Article

Parks, G.S., Jones, S.E.
Nigger: A critical race realist analysis of the n-word within hate crimes law
(2008) Journal of Criminal Law and Criminology, 98 (4), pp. 1305-1352.
LANGUAGE OF ORIGINAL DOCUMENT: English
DOCUMENT TYPE: Review

Gustafson, R.

Drifters and the dancing mad: The public school music curriculum and the fabrication of boundaries for participation
(2008) Curriculum Inquiry, 38 (3), pp. 267-297.
LANGUAGE OF ORIGINAL DOCUMENT: English
DOCUMENT TYPE: Article

Baxter, V.K., Marina, P.
Cultural meaning and hip-hop fashion in the African-American male youth subculture of New Orleans
(2008) Journal of Youth Studies, 11 (2), pp. 93-113.
LANGUAGE OF ORIGINAL DOCUMENT: English
DOCUMENT TYPE: Article

Patrick, B.A.
Vikings and rappers: The icelandic sagas hip-hop across 8 mile
(2008) Journal of Popular Culture, 41 (2), pp. 281-305.
LANGUAGE OF ORIGINAL DOCUMENT: English
DOCUMENT TYPE: Article

Motley, C.M., Henderson, G.R.
The global hip-hop Diaspora: Understanding the culture
(2008) Journal of Business Research, 61 (3), pp. 243-253.
LANGUAGE OF ORIGINAL DOCUMENT: English

DOCUMENT TYPE: Article

Huff, L.C., Smith, S.M.
Cross-Cultural Business Research: Introduction to the special issue
(2008) Journal of Business Research, 61 (3), pp. 179-182.
LANGUAGE OF ORIGINAL DOCUMENT: English
DOCUMENT TYPE: Article

Gartner, W.B.
Entrepreneurship-Hop
(2008) Entrepreneurship: Theory and Practice, 32 (2), pp. 361-368.
LANGUAGE OF ORIGINAL DOCUMENT: English
DOCUMENT TYPE: Article

Baker, S., Cohen, B.M.Z.
From snuggling and snogging to sampling and scratching: Girls' nonparticipation in community-based music activities
(2008) Youth and Society, 39 (3), pp. 316-339.
LANGUAGE OF ORIGINAL DOCUMENT: English
DOCUMENT TYPE: Article

Zweigenhaft, R.L.
A Do Re Mi Encore: A Closer Look at the Personality Correlates of Music Preferences
(2008) Journal of Individual Differences, 29 (1), pp. 45-55.
LANGUAGE OF ORIGINAL DOCUMENT: English
DOCUMENT TYPE: Article

Rivera, R.Z.
Between Blackness and Latinidad in the Hip Hop Zone
(2008) A Companion to Latina/o Studies, pp. 351-362.
PUBLISHER: Wiley Blackwell
LANGUAGE OF ORIGINAL DOCUMENT: English
DOCUMENT TYPE: Book Chapter

Primack, B.A., Dalton, M.A., Carroll, M.V., Agarwal, A.A., Fine, M.J.

Content analysis of tobacco, alcohol, and other drugs in popular music
(2008) Archives of Pediatrics and Adolescent Medicine, 162 (2), pp. 169-175.
LANGUAGE OF ORIGINAL DOCUMENT: English
DOCUMENT TYPE: Article
ACCESS TYPE: Open Access

Meisel, P.
From Bebop to Hip Hop: American Music After 1950
(2008) A Concise Companion to Postwar American Literature and Culture, pp. 95-109.
PUBLISHER: John Wiley and Sons
LANGUAGE OF ORIGINAL DOCUMENT: English
DOCUMENT TYPE: Book Chapter

Manivet, B., Richelieu, A.
Dangerous liaisons: how can sports brands capitalise on the Hip Hop movement
(2008) International Journal of Sport Management and Marketing, 3 (1-2), pp. 140-161.
LANGUAGE OF ORIGINAL DOCUMENT: English
DOCUMENT TYPE: Article

Ovalle, P.
Urban sensualidad: Jennifer Lopez, Flashdance and the MTV hip-hop re-generation
(2008) Women and Performance, 18 (3), pp. 253-268.
LANGUAGE OF ORIGINAL DOCUMENT: English
DOCUMENT TYPE: Article

Schlund-Vials, C.J.
A transnational hip hop nation: Prach, cambodia, and memorialising the killing fields
(2008) Life Writing, 5 (1), pp. 11-27.
LANGUAGE OF ORIGINAL DOCUMENT: English
DOCUMENT TYPE: Article

Cutler, C.
Brooklyn style: Hip-hop markers and racial affiliation among European immigrants in New York City
(2008) International Journal of Bilingualism, 12 (1-2), pp. 7-24.
PUBLISHER: Kingston Press Services Ltd
LANGUAGE OF ORIGINAL DOCUMENT: English
DOCUMENT TYPE: Conference Paper

Cobb, W.
To the Break of Dawn: A freestyle on the hip hop aesthetic
(2008) To the Break of Dawn: A Freestyle on the Hip Hop Aesthetic, pp. 1-199.
PUBLISHER: New York University Press
LANGUAGE OF ORIGINAL DOCUMENT: English
DOCUMENT TYPE: Book

Shevy, M.
Music genre as cognitive schema: Extramusical associations with country and hip-hop music
(2008) Psychology of Music, 36 (4), pp. 477-498.
PUBLISHER: SAGE Publications Ltd
LANGUAGE OF ORIGINAL DOCUMENT: English
DOCUMENT TYPE: Article

Pardue, D.
Ideologies of marginality in Brazilian hip hop
(2008) Ideologies of Marginality in Brazilian Hip Hop, pp. 1-210.
PUBLISHER: Palgrave Macmillan
LANGUAGE OF ORIGINAL DOCUMENT: English
DOCUMENT TYPE: Book

McCune, J.Q., Jr.
"Out" in the club: The down low, hip-hop, and the architexture of black masculinity
(2008) Text and Performance Quarterly, 28 (3), pp. 298-314.
LANGUAGE OF ORIGINAL DOCUMENT: English
DOCUMENT TYPE: Article

Lashua, B.D., Kelly, J.

Rhythms in the concrete: Re-imagining relationships between space, race, and mediated urban youth cultures
(2008) Leisure/ Loisir, 32 (2), pp. 461-487.
LANGUAGE OF ORIGINAL DOCUMENT: English
DOCUMENT TYPE: Article

Grealy, L.
Negotiating cultural authenticity in hip-hop: Mimicry, whiteness and Eminem
(2008) Continuum, 22 (6), pp. 851-865.
PUBLISHER: Routledge
LANGUAGE OF ORIGINAL DOCUMENT: English
DOCUMENT TYPE: Conference Paper

Preston, G.C.-H.
My pen rides the paper: Hip-hop, the technology of writing and Nas's Illmatic
(2008) Journal of Popular Music Studies, 20 (3), pp. 261-275.
PUBLISHER: University of California Press
LANGUAGE OF ORIGINAL DOCUMENT: English
DOCUMENT TYPE: Article

Miranda, D., Claes, M.
Personality traits, music preferences and depression in adolescence
(2008) International Journal of Adolescence and Youth, 14 (3), pp. 277-298.
    PUBLISHER: A B Academic Publishers
    LANGUAGE OF ORIGINAL DOCUMENT: English
    DOCUMENT TYPE: Article
    ACCESS TYPE: Open Access

Russell, E.
Writing on the wall: The form, function and meaning of tagging
(2008) Journal of Occupational Science, 15 (2), pp. 87-97.
    LANGUAGE OF ORIGINAL DOCUMENT: English
    DOCUMENT TYPE: Article

Baxendale, S.
The representation of epilepsy in popular music
(2008) Epilepsy and Behavior, 12 (1), pp. 165-169.
    LANGUAGE OF ORIGINAL DOCUMENT: English
    DOCUMENT TYPE: Review

Gary, H.
History of texas music
(2008) History of Texas Music, pp. 1-304.
    PUBLISHER: Texas A and M University Press
    LANGUAGE OF ORIGINAL DOCUMENT: English
    DOCUMENT TYPE: Book

Primack, B.A., Gold, M.A., Schwarz, E.B., Dalton, M.A.
Degrading and non-degrading sex in popular music: A content analysis
(2008) Public Health Reports, 123 (5), pp. 593-600.
    PUBLISHER: Association of Schools of Public Health
    LANGUAGE OF ORIGINAL DOCUMENT: English
    DOCUMENT TYPE: Article

Webb, P.

Exploring the networked worlds of popular music: Milieu cultures
(2007) Exploring the Networked Worlds of Popular Music: Milieu Cultures, pp. 1-277.
PUBLISHER: Routledge Taylor & Francis Group
LANGUAGE OF ORIGINAL DOCUMENT: English
DOCUMENT TYPE: Book

Drissel, D.
Online jihadism for the hip-hop generation: Mobilizing diasporic muslim youth in cyberspace
(2007) International Journal of Interdisciplinary Social Sciences, 2 (4), pp. 7-19.
LANGUAGE OF ORIGINAL DOCUMENT: English
DOCUMENT TYPE: Article

Putnam, M.T., Littlejohn, J.T.
National Socialism with Fler? German hip hop from the right
(2007) Popular Music and Society, 30 (4), pp. 453-468.
LANGUAGE OF ORIGINAL DOCUMENT: English
DOCUMENT TYPE: Article

Dowdy, M.
Live hip hop, collective agency, and "acting in concert"
(2007) Popular Music and Society, 30 (1), pp. 75-91.
LANGUAGE OF ORIGINAL DOCUMENT: English
DOCUMENT TYPE: Article

Kato, M.T.
From Kung Fu to hip hop: Globalization, revolution, and popular culture
(2007) From Kung Fu to Hip Hop: Globalization, Revolution, and Popular Culture, pp. 1-267.
PUBLISHER: State University of New York Press
LANGUAGE OF ORIGINAL DOCUMENT: English
DOCUMENT TYPE: Book

Johnson, L.D.
The art of the dis: Hip-Hop's battle royale

(2007) Etiquette: Reflections on Contemporary Comportment, pp. 17-31.
PUBLISHER: State University of New York Press
LANGUAGE OF ORIGINAL DOCUMENT: English
DOCUMENT TYPE: Book Chapter

Santoro, M., Solaroli, M.
Authors and rappers: Italian hip hop and the shifting boundaries of canzone d'autore
(2007) Popular Music, 26 (3), pp. 463-488.
LANGUAGE OF ORIGINAL DOCUMENT: English
DOCUMENT TYPE: Review

Ferrari, A.
Hip-hop in Nairobi: Recognition of an international movement and the main means of expression for the urban youth in poor residential areas
(2007) Songs and Politics in Eastern Africa, pp. 107-128.
PUBLISHER: African Books Collective
LANGUAGE OF ORIGINAL DOCUMENT: English
DOCUMENT TYPE: Book Chapter

Bancet, A.
Formation of a popular music: Hip-hop in Tanzania: Emphasis on its social and political engagement
(2007) Songs and Politics in Eastern Africa, pp. 315-354.
PUBLISHER: African Books Collective
LANGUAGE OF ORIGINAL DOCUMENT: English
DOCUMENT TYPE: Book Chapter

Ntarangwi, M.
Hip-hop, westernization and gender in East Africa
(2007) Songs and Politics in Eastern Africa, pp. 273-302.
PUBLISHER: African Books Collective
LANGUAGE OF ORIGINAL DOCUMENT: English
DOCUMENT TYPE: Book Chapter

Perullo, A.

'Here's a little something local': An early history of hip hop in Dar es Salaam 1984-1997

(2007) Dar es Salaam: Histories from an Emerging African Metropolis, pp. 250-272.
PUBLISHER: African Books Collective
LANGUAGE OF ORIGINAL DOCUMENT: English
DOCUMENT TYPE: Book Chapter

Wisner, H.
Technique: Crash course: Hip hop
(2007) Dance Magazine, 81 (10), pp. 82-87.
LANGUAGE OF ORIGINAL DOCUMENT: English
DOCUMENT TYPE: Review

Condry, I.
Yellow B-Boys, black culture, and hip-hop in Japan: Toward a transnational cultural politics of race
(2007) Positions, 15 (3), pp. 637-671+673.
LANGUAGE OF ORIGINAL DOCUMENT: English
DOCUMENT TYPE: Article

Myer, L., Kleck, C.
From independent to corporate: A political economic analysis of rap billboard Toppers
(2007) Popular Music and Society, 30 (2), pp. 137-148.

LANGUAGE OF ORIGINAL DOCUMENT: English
DOCUMENT TYPE: Article

Harper, G.
Breakin' the mould
(2007) Dancing Times, 97 (1161), pp. 12-16.
LANGUAGE OF ORIGINAL DOCUMENT: English
DOCUMENT TYPE: Review

Amokrane, S.
Tactikollectif: Action culturelle et engagement politique
(2007) Empan, 67 (3), pp. 46-49.
LANGUAGE OF ORIGINAL DOCUMENT: French
DOCUMENT TYPE: Article

Monteyne, K.B.
The sound of the south bronx :Youth culture, genre, and performance in charlie ahearn's wild style
(2007) Youth Culture in Global Cinema, pp. 87-105.
PUBLISHER: University of Texas Press
LANGUAGE OF ORIGINAL DOCUMENT: English
DOCUMENT TYPE: Book Chapter

Fukuchi, K.
Multi-track scratch player on a multi-touch sensing device
(2007) Lecture Notes in Computer Science (including subseries Lecture Notes in Artificial Intelligence and Lecture Notes in Bioinformatics), 4740 LNCS, pp. 211-218.
CONFERENCE NAME: 6th International Conference of Entertainment Computing, ICEC 2007
CONFERENCE DATE: 15 September 2007 through 17 September 2007
CONFERENCE LOCATION: Shanghai
LANGUAGE OF ORIGINAL DOCUMENT: English
DOCUMENT TYPE: Conference Paper

Szabó-Gilinger, E.
Rap Francophone: Création d'identité culturelle in action

(2007) Verbum, 9 (2), pp. 231-243.
LANGUAGE OF ORIGINAL DOCUMENT: French
DOCUMENT TYPE: Article

Scapp, R., Seitz, B.
Etiquette: Reflections on contemporary comportment
(2007) Etiquette: Reflections on Contemporary Comportment, pp. 1-260.
PUBLISHER: State University of New York Press
LANGUAGE OF ORIGINAL DOCUMENT: English
DOCUMENT TYPE: Book

Pennycook, A.
'The rotation gets thick. the constraints get thin': Creativity, recontextualization, and difference
(2007) Applied Linguistics, 28 (4), pp. 579-596.
LANGUAGE OF ORIGINAL DOCUMENT: English
DOCUMENT TYPE: Article

Barksdale, M.C., Livingston, S.T.
"Race Rebels": From Indigenous Insurgency to Hip-Hop Mania
(2007) A Companion to African American History, pp. 512-528.
PUBLISHER: John Wiley and Sons
LANGUAGE OF ORIGINAL DOCUMENT: English
DOCUMENT TYPE: Book Chapter

Hill, M.L.
Toward a pedagogy of the popular: Bourdieu, hip-hop, and out-of-school literacies
(2007) Pierre Bourdieu and Literacy Education, pp. 136-161.
PUBLISHER: Routledge Taylor & Francis Group
LANGUAGE OF ORIGINAL DOCUMENT: English
DOCUMENT TYPE: Book Chapter

Muñoz-Laboy, M., Weinstein, H., Parker, R.
The Hip-Hop club scene: Gender, grinding and sex
(2007) Culture, Health and Sexuality, 9 (6), pp. 615-628.
LANGUAGE OF ORIGINAL DOCUMENT: English

DOCUMENT TYPE: Article

Richardson, E.
'She was workin like foreal': Critical literacy and discourse practices of African American females in the age of hip hop
(2007) Discourse and Society, 18 (6), pp. 789-809.
LANGUAGE OF ORIGINAL DOCUMENT: English
DOCUMENT TYPE: Article

Chang, J.
It's a hip-hop world
(2007) Foreign Policy, (163), pp. 58-65.
LANGUAGE OF ORIGINAL DOCUMENT: English
DOCUMENT TYPE: Review

Watkins, S.C.
Why hip-hop is like no other
(2007) Foreign Policy, (163), p. 63.
LANGUAGE OF ORIGINAL DOCUMENT: English
DOCUMENT TYPE: Note

Nisker, J.
"Only God can judge me": Tupac Shakur, the legal system, and lyrical subversion
(2007) Journal of Criminal Justice and Popular Culture, 14 (2), pp. 176-196.
LANGUAGE OF ORIGINAL DOCUMENT: English
DOCUMENT TYPE: Article

Gibbons, W.C.
From the streets to academia: A librarian's guide to hip-hop culture
(2007) Collection Building, 26 (4), pp. 119-126.
LANGUAGE OF ORIGINAL DOCUMENT: English
DOCUMENT TYPE: Article

Wong, W.H., Huang, J.

Outdoor pop concert sound control: Open-air concert in the heart of Hong Kong

(2007) Huanan Ligong Daxue Xuebao/Journal of South China University of Technology (Natural Science), 35 (SUPPL.), pp. 144-149.

LANGUAGE OF ORIGINAL DOCUMENT: English
DOCUMENT TYPE: Article

Kaya, A.
German-Turkish transnational space: A separate space of their own
(2007) German Studies Review, 30 (3), pp. 483-502.
LANGUAGE OF ORIGINAL DOCUMENT: English
DOCUMENT TYPE: Article

Cheng, Z.
When mother tongues meet music
(2007) Taiwan Review, 57 (10), pp. 52-57.
LANGUAGE OF ORIGINAL DOCUMENT: English
DOCUMENT TYPE: Article

Crawford, C.
A little bit of history repeating: Denim today
(2007) AATCC Review, 7 (10), pp. 22-25.

LANGUAGE OF ORIGINAL DOCUMENT: English
DOCUMENT TYPE: Article

Stephens, D.P., Few, A.L.
**Hip Hop honey or video ho: African American preadolescents'
understanding of female sexual scripts in hip hop culture**
(2007) Sexuality and Culture, 11 (4), pp. 48-69.
LANGUAGE OF ORIGINAL DOCUMENT: English
DOCUMENT TYPE: Review

Moehn, F.
Music, citizenship, and violence in postdictatorship Brazil
(2007) Latin American Music Review - Revista de Musica
Latinoamericana, 28 (2), pp. 181-219.
LANGUAGE OF ORIGINAL DOCUMENT: English
DOCUMENT TYPE: Article

Baker, S., Homan, S.
**Rap, recidivism and the creative self: A popular music programme
for young offenders in detention**
(2007) Journal of Youth Studies, 10 (4), pp. 459-476.
LANGUAGE OF ORIGINAL DOCUMENT: English
DOCUMENT TYPE: Article

Cheng, C.H.
A study | Zoot Suit | and Africa American street styles
(2007) Taiwan Textile Research Journal, 17 (1), pp. 39-46.
LANGUAGE OF ORIGINAL DOCUMENT: Chinese
DOCUMENT TYPE: Article

Greenfield, D.
**What's the deal with the white middle-aged guy teaching hip-hop?
Lessons in popular culture, positionality and pedagogy**
(2007) Pedagogy, Culture and Society, 15 (2), pp. 229-243.
LANGUAGE OF ORIGINAL DOCUMENT: English
DOCUMENT TYPE: Article

Munby, J.
Signifyin' cinema: Rudy Ray Moore and the quality of badness
(2007) Journal for Cultural Research, 11 (3), pp. 203-219.
LANGUAGE OF ORIGINAL DOCUMENT: English
DOCUMENT TYPE: Review

Irobi, E.
What they came with: Carnival and the persistence of African Performance aesthetics in the Diaspora
(2007) Family Journal, 15 (3), pp. 896-913.
LANGUAGE OF ORIGINAL DOCUMENT: English
DOCUMENT TYPE: Article

Monk-Turner, E., Kouts, T., Parris, K., Webb, C.
Gender role stereotyping in advertisements on three radio stations: Does musical genre make a difference?
(2007) Journal of Gender Studies, 16 (2), pp. 173-182.
LANGUAGE OF ORIGINAL DOCUMENT: English
DOCUMENT TYPE: Article

Webb, P.
Hip hop's musicians and audiences in the local musical 'milieu'
(2007) Youth Cultures: Scenes, Subcultures and Tribes, pp. 175-187.
PUBLISHER: Routledge Taylor & Francis Group
LANGUAGE OF ORIGINAL DOCUMENT: English
DOCUMENT TYPE: Book Chapter

Huq, R.
Resistance or incorporation?: Youth policy making and hip hop culture
(2007) Youth Cultures: Scenes, Subcultures and Tribes, pp. 79-92.
PUBLISHER: Routledge Taylor & Francis Group
LANGUAGE OF ORIGINAL DOCUMENT: English
DOCUMENT TYPE: Book Chapter

Pardue, D.
Hip hop as pedagogy: A look into "heaven" and "soul" in São Paulo, Brazil

(2007) Anthropological Quarterly, 80 (3), pp. 673-709.
LANGUAGE OF ORIGINAL DOCUMENT: English
DOCUMENT TYPE: Review

Kim, S., Kim, J.
Mood after various brief exercise and sport modes: Aerobics, hip-hop dancing, ice skating, and body conditioning
(2007) Perceptual and Motor Skills, 104 (3 II), pp. 1265-1270.
LANGUAGE OF ORIGINAL DOCUMENT: English
DOCUMENT TYPE: Article

Cole, M.D.
Hip hopping into fashion's mainstream
(2007) Knitting International, 113 (1347), pp. 32-34.
LANGUAGE OF ORIGINAL DOCUMENT: English
DOCUMENT TYPE: Article

Leppänen, S.
Youth language in media contexts: Insights into the functions of English in Finland
(2007) World Englishes, 26 (2), pp. 149-169.
LANGUAGE OF ORIGINAL DOCUMENT: English
DOCUMENT TYPE: Article

Xie, P.F., Osumare, H., Ibrahim, A.
Gazing the hood: Hip-Hop as tourism attraction
(2007) Tourism Management, 28 (2), pp. 452-460.
LANGUAGE OF ORIGINAL DOCUMENT: English
DOCUMENT TYPE: Article

Morgado, M.A.
The semiotics of extraordinary dress: A structural analysis and interpretation of hip-hop style
(2007) Clothing and Textiles Research Journal, 25 (2), pp. 131-155.
LANGUAGE OF ORIGINAL DOCUMENT: English
DOCUMENT TYPE: Article

Sensui, H., Imamura, Y., Fujimoto, T., Nagamatsu, T.
Effects of goal oriented dance exercise on mood in healthy young adults and schizophrenic patients
(2007) Bulletin of the Physical Fitness Research Institute, (105), pp. 11-16.

LANGUAGE OF ORIGINAL DOCUMENT: Japanese
DOCUMENT TYPE: Article

Stokes, C.E.
Representin' in cyberspace: Sexual scripts, self-definition, and hip hop culture in Black American adolescent girls' home pages
(2007) Culture, Health and Sexuality, 9 (2), pp. 169-184.
LANGUAGE OF ORIGINAL DOCUMENT: English
DOCUMENT TYPE: Article

Cutler, C.
The co-construction of whiteness in an MC battle
(2007) Pragmatics, 17 (1), pp. 19-22.
LANGUAGE OF ORIGINAL DOCUMENT: English
DOCUMENT TYPE: Article

Yap, T.
Incorporating America
(2007) Sportswear International, (211), pp. 50-51.
LANGUAGE OF ORIGINAL DOCUMENT: English
DOCUMENT TYPE: Article

Verkooijen, K.T., De Vries, N.K., Nielsen, G.A.
Youth crowds and substance use: The impact of perceived group norm and multiple group identification
(2007) Psychology of Addictive Behaviors, 21 (1), pp. 55-61.
LANGUAGE OF ORIGINAL DOCUMENT: English
DOCUMENT TYPE: Article

Oesterreich, H.
From 'crisis' to activist: The everyday freedom legacy of black feminisms
(2007) Race Ethnicity and Education, 10 (1), pp. 1-20.
LANGUAGE OF ORIGINAL DOCUMENT: English
DOCUMENT TYPE: Article

Campbell, K.E.
There goes the neighborhood: Hip hop creepir' on a come up at the U
(2007) College Composition and Communication, 58 (3), pp. 325-344.
LANGUAGE OF ORIGINAL DOCUMENT: English
DOCUMENT TYPE: Article

Stephens, D.P., Few, A.L.
The effects of images of African American women in hip hop on early adolescents' attitudes toward physical attractiveness and interpersonal relationships
(2007) Sex Roles, 56 (3-4), pp. 251-264.
LANGUAGE OF ORIGINAL DOCUMENT: English
DOCUMENT TYPE: Article

Sköld, D., Rehn, A.
Makin' it, by keeping it real: Street talk, rap music, and the

forgotten entrepreneurship from "the 'hood"
(2007) Group and Organization Management, 32 (1), pp. 50-78.
LANGUAGE OF ORIGINAL DOCUMENT: English
DOCUMENT TYPE: Article

Hall, H.R.
Poetic Expressions: Students of Color Express Resiliency Through Metaphors and Similes
(2007) Journal of Advanced Academics, 18 (2), pp. 216-244.
PUBLISHER: SAGE Publications Ltd
LANGUAGE OF ORIGINAL DOCUMENT: English
DOCUMENT TYPE: Article

Gelder, K.
Subcultures: Cultural histories and social practice
(2007) Subcultures: Cultural Histories and Social Practice, pp. 1-188.
PUBLISHER: Routledge Taylor & Francis Group
LANGUAGE OF ORIGINAL DOCUMENT: English
DOCUMENT TYPE: Book

Sharpley-Whiting, T.
Pimps Up, Ho's Down: Hip Hop's Hold on Young Black Women
(2007) Pimps Up, Ho's Down: Hip Hop's Hold on Young Black Women, pp. 1-200.
PUBLISHER: New York University Press
LANGUAGE OF ORIGINAL DOCUMENT: English
DOCUMENT TYPE: Book

Smith, S.
The process of 'collective creation' in the composition of UK hip-hop turntable team routines
(2007) Organised Sound, 12 (1), pp. 79-87.
LANGUAGE OF ORIGINAL DOCUMENT: English
DOCUMENT TYPE: Article

Khan, K.
Cultural authenticity or cultural contamination: American musical influences on south african hip-hop culture

(2007) Muziki, 4 (1), pp. 3-11.
LANGUAGE OF ORIGINAL DOCUMENT: English
DOCUMENT TYPE: Article

Schloss, J.
From Mambo to Hip Hop: A South Bronx Story by Henry Chalfant (Dir.)
(2007) Journal of Popular Music Studies, 19 (4), pp. 399-402.
LANGUAGE OF ORIGINAL DOCUMENT: English
DOCUMENT TYPE: Article

Hughey, M.W.
From black power to hip hop: Racism, nationalism, and feminism by patricia hill collins
(2007) Souls, 9 (2), pp. 187-189.
LANGUAGE OF ORIGINAL DOCUMENT: English
DOCUMENT TYPE: Article

Miyakawa, F.M.
Turntablature: Notation, legitimization, and the art of the hip-hop DJ
(2007) American Music, 25 (1), pp. 81-105.
PUBLISHER: University of Illinois Press
LANGUAGE OF ORIGINAL DOCUMENT: English
DOCUMENT TYPE: Article

Kahf, U.
Arabic Hip Hop: Claims of Authenticity and Identity of a New Genre
(2007) Journal of Popular Music Studies, 19 (4), pp. 359-385.
LANGUAGE OF ORIGINAL DOCUMENT: English
DOCUMENT TYPE: Article

Khabeer, S.A.
Rep that Islam: The rhyme and reason of American Islamic hip hop
(2007) Muslim World, 97 (1), pp. 125-141.
PUBLISHER: Blackwell Publishing Ltd

LANGUAGE OF ORIGINAL DOCUMENT: English
DOCUMENT TYPE: Review

Quintero Rivera, Á.G.
Migration, ethnicity, and interactions between the United States and Hispanic Caribbean popular culture

(2007) Latin American Perspectives, 34 (1), pp. 83-93.
  LANGUAGE OF ORIGINAL DOCUMENT: English
  DOCUMENT TYPE: Article

The beat
(2007) The Beat, 9781604733433, pp. 1-289.
PUBLISHER: University Press of Mississippi
LANGUAGE OF ORIGINAL DOCUMENT: English
DOCUMENT TYPE: Book

Damasceno, F.J.G.
As cidades da juventude em Fortaleza
(2007) Revista Brasileira de Historia, 27 (53), .
LANGUAGE OF ORIGINAL DOCUMENT: Portuguese
DOCUMENT TYPE: Article

Irobi, E.
What They Came With: Carnival and the Persistence of African Performance Aesthetics in the Diaspora
(2007) Journal of Black Studies, 37 (6), pp. 896-913.
LANGUAGE OF ORIGINAL DOCUMENT: English
DOCUMENT TYPE: Article

Tak, Y.R., An, J.Y., Kim, Y.A., Woo, H.Y.
The effects of a physical activity-behavior modification combined intervention(PABM-intervention) on metabolic risk factors in overweight and obese elementary school children
(2007) Taehan Kanho Hakhoe chi, 37 (6), pp. 902-913.
LANGUAGE OF ORIGINAL DOCUMENT: Korean
DOCUMENT TYPE: Article
ACCESS TYPE: Open Access

Shandu, T.P.
Pitch black language: The quest for language purity in isizulu popular music
(2007) Muziki, 4 (2), pp. 263-277.
LANGUAGE OF ORIGINAL DOCUMENT: English
DOCUMENT TYPE: Article

Jordà, S.
Interactivity and live computer music
(2007) The Cambridge Companion to Electronic Music, pp. 89-106.
PUBLISHER: Cambridge University Press
LANGUAGE OF ORIGINAL DOCUMENT: English
DOCUMENT TYPE: Book Chapter

Sá, L.
Cyberspace neighbourhood: The virtual construction of Capão Redondo
(2007) Latin American Cyberculture and Cyberliterature, pp. 123-139.
PUBLISHER: Liverpool University Press
LANGUAGE OF ORIGINAL DOCUMENT: English
DOCUMENT TYPE: Book Chapter

Hutnyk, J.
Pantomime Terror: Diasporic Music in a Time of War
(2007) Journal of Creative Communications, 2 (2), pp. 123-141.
LANGUAGE OF ORIGINAL DOCUMENT: English
DOCUMENT TYPE: Article

Hay, S.A.
Joe Turner's come and gone
(2007) The Cambridge Companion to August Wilson, pp. 89-101.
PUBLISHER: Cambridge University Press
LANGUAGE OF ORIGINAL DOCUMENT: English
DOCUMENT TYPE: Book Chapter

Buhler, S.M.
Musical Shakespeares: Attending to Ophelia, Juliet, and Desdemona
(2007) The Cambridge Companion to Shakespeare and Popular Culture, pp. 150-174.
PUBLISHER: Cambridge University Press
LANGUAGE OF ORIGINAL DOCUMENT: English
DOCUMENT TYPE: Book Chapter

Pennycook, A.
Global englishes and transcultural flows
(2006) Global Englishes and Transcultural Flows, pp. 1-189.
PUBLISHER: Routledge Taylor & Francis Group
LANGUAGE OF ORIGINAL DOCUMENT: English
DOCUMENT TYPE: Book

Rodriquez, J.
Color-blind ideology and the cultural appropriation of hip-hop
(2006) Journal of Contemporary Ethnography, 35 (6), pp. 645-668.
LANGUAGE OF ORIGINAL DOCUMENT: English
DOCUMENT TYPE: Article

Lewis, J., Assogba, Y.
Taking sides: Dynamic text and hip-hop performance
(2006) Proceedings of the 14th Annual ACM International Conference

on Multimedia, MM 2006, pp. 744-747.
SPONSORS: ACM Special Interest Group on Multimedia
CONFERENCE NAME: 14th Annual ACM International Conference
on Multimedia, MM 2006
CONFERENCE DATE: 23 October 2006 through 27 October 2006
CONFERENCE LOCATION: Santa Barbara, CA
LANGUAGE OF ORIGINAL DOCUMENT: English
DOCUMENT TYPE: Conference Paper

Harrison, A.K.
'Cheaper than a CD, plus we really mean it': Bay Area underground hip hop tapes as subcultural artefacts
(2006) Popular Music, 25 (2), pp. 283-301.
LANGUAGE OF ORIGINAL DOCUMENT: English
DOCUMENT TYPE: Review

Squires, C.R., Kohn-Wood, L.P., Chavous, T., Carter, P.L.
Evaluating agency and responsibility in gendered violence: African American youth talk about violence and hip hop
(2006) Sex Roles, 55 (11-12), pp. 725-737.
LANGUAGE OF ORIGINAL DOCUMENT: English
DOCUMENT TYPE: Article

Lashua, B.D.
"Just another native?" Soundscapes, chorasters, and borderlands in Edmonton, Alberta, Canada
(2006) Cultural Studies - Critical Methodologies, 6 (3), pp. 391-410.
LANGUAGE OF ORIGINAL DOCUMENT: English
DOCUMENT TYPE: Article

Wang, O.
These are the breaks: Hip-hop and afroasian cultural (dis)connections
(2006) AfroAsian Encounters: Culture, History, Politics, pp. 146-164.
PUBLISHER: NYU Press
LANGUAGE OF ORIGINAL DOCUMENT: English
DOCUMENT TYPE: Book Chapter

Whaley, D.E.
BLack Bodies/Yellow Masks: The orientalist aesthetic in hip-hop and black visual culture
(2006) AfroAsian Encounters: Culture, History, Politics, pp. 188-203.
PUBLISHER: NYU Press
LANGUAGE OF ORIGINAL DOCUMENT: English
DOCUMENT TYPE: Book Chapter

Gregory, K.
Hip hop in London
(2006) Dancing Times, 96 (1147), p. 47.
LANGUAGE OF ORIGINAL DOCUMENT: English
DOCUMENT TYPE: Article

Monaghan, T.
Hip hop dance styles
(2006) Dancing Times, 97 (1157), p. 101.
LANGUAGE OF ORIGINAL DOCUMENT: English
DOCUMENT TYPE: Article

Hanlon, K.
Hip hop from head to toe ...June is bustin' out all over!
(2006) Dance Magazine, 80 (6), p. 66.
LANGUAGE OF ORIGINAL DOCUMENT: English

DOCUMENT TYPE: Note

Hess, M.
From bricks to billboards: Hip-hop autobiography
(2006) Mosaic, 39 (1), .
LANGUAGE OF ORIGINAL DOCUMENT: English
DOCUMENT TYPE: Article

Pisares, E.H.
Do you mis(recognize) me: Filipina Americans in popular music and the problem of invisibility
(2006) Positively No Filipinos Allowed: Building Communities and Discourse, pp. 172-198.
PUBLISHER: Temple University Press
LANGUAGE OF ORIGINAL DOCUMENT: English
DOCUMENT TYPE: Book Chapter

Chung, M.-B., Ko, I.-J.
Representative melodies retrieval using digital signal processing of audio
(2006) Proceedings - 2006 International Conference on Hybrid Information Technology, ICHIT 2006, 2, art. no. 4021215, pp. 185-190.
CONFERENCE NAME: 2006 International Conference on Hybrid Information Technology, ICHIT 2006
CONFERENCE DATE: 9 November 2006 through 11 November 2006
CONFERENCE LOCATION: Cheju Island
LANGUAGE OF ORIGINAL DOCUMENT: English
DOCUMENT TYPE: Conference Paper

Jackson II, R.L.
Scripting the black masculine body: Identity, discourse, and racial politics in popular media
(2006) Scripting the Black Masculine Body: Identity, Discourse, and Racial Politics in Popular Media, pp. 1-179.
PUBLISHER: State University of New York Press
LANGUAGE OF ORIGINAL DOCUMENT: English
DOCUMENT TYPE: Book

North, A.C., Hargreaves, D.J.
Problem music and self-harming
(2006) Suicide and Life-Threatening Behavior, 36 (5), pp. 582-590.
LANGUAGE OF ORIGINAL DOCUMENT: English
DOCUMENT TYPE: Article

Manuel, P., Marshall, W.
The riddim method: Aesthetics, practice, and ownership in Jamaican dancehall
(2006) Popular Music, 25 (3), pp. 447-470.
LANGUAGE OF ORIGINAL DOCUMENT: English
DOCUMENT TYPE: Review

Callahan, A.D.
The talking book: African Americans and the Bible
(2006) The Talking Book: African Americans and the Bible, pp. 1-286.
PUBLISHER: Yale University Press
LANGUAGE OF ORIGINAL DOCUMENT: English
DOCUMENT TYPE: Book

Fairley, J.
Dancing back to front: Regeton, sexuality, gender and transnationalism in Cuba
(2006) Popular Music, 25 (3), pp. 471-488.
LANGUAGE OF ORIGINAL DOCUMENT: English
DOCUMENT TYPE: Review

Ripani, R.J.
The new blue music: Changes in rhythm and blues, 1950-1999
(2006) The New Blue Music: Changes in Rhythm and Blues, 1950-1999, pp. 1-261.
PUBLISHER: University Press of Mississippi
LANGUAGE OF ORIGINAL DOCUMENT: English
DOCUMENT TYPE: Book

Kimminich, E.
Citoyen or stranger? Exclusion and cultural autonomy in the

French banlieue [Citoyen oder fremder? Ausgrenzung und kulturelle autonomie in der Französischen banlieue]
(2006) Archiv fur Sozialgeschichte, 46, pp. 505-538+796+805-806.
LANGUAGE OF ORIGINAL DOCUMENT: German
DOCUMENT TYPE: Article

Pope, S.W.
Decentering "race" and (re)presenting "black" performance in sport history: Basketball and jazz in American culture, 1920-1950
(2006) Deconstructing Sport History: A Postmodern Analysis, pp. 147-177.
PUBLISHER: State University of New York Press
LANGUAGE OF ORIGINAL DOCUMENT: English
DOCUMENT TYPE: Book Chapter

Stovall, D.
We can relate: Hip-hop culture, critical pedagogy, and the secondary classroom
(2006) Urban Education, 41 (6), pp. 585-602.
LANGUAGE OF ORIGINAL DOCUMENT: English
DOCUMENT TYPE: Article

Sheridan, E.
Conservative implications of the irrelevance of racism in contemporary African American cinema
(2006) Journal of Black Studies, 37 (2), pp. 177-192.
LANGUAGE OF ORIGINAL DOCUMENT: English
DOCUMENT TYPE: Review

Polley-Edmunds, P.K., Williams, E.L.
The globalisation of the hip hop market
(2006) International Journal of Management and Decision Making, 7 (5), pp. 557-570.
LANGUAGE OF ORIGINAL DOCUMENT: English
DOCUMENT TYPE: Article

Hill, M.L.
Representin(g): Negotiating multiple roles and identities in the

field and behind the desk
(2006) Qualitative Inquiry, 12 (5), pp. 926-949.
LANGUAGE OF ORIGINAL DOCUMENT: English
DOCUMENT TYPE: Article

Hafez, N., Ling, P.M.
Finding the Kool Mixx: How Brown and Williamson used music

marketing to sell cigarettes
(2006) Tobacco Control, 15 (5), pp. 359-366.
LANGUAGE OF ORIGINAL DOCUMENT: English
DOCUMENT TYPE: Article

Fox, K.M., Klaiber, E.
Listening for a leisure remix
(2006) Leisure Sciences, 28 (5), pp. 411-430.
LANGUAGE OF ORIGINAL DOCUMENT: English
DOCUMENT TYPE: Article

Brown, T.J.
Welcome to the terrordome: Exploring the contradictions of a hip-hop black masculinity
(2006) Progressive Black Masculinities, pp. 191-213.
PUBLISHER: Routledge Taylor & Francis Group

LANGUAGE OF ORIGINAL DOCUMENT: English
DOCUMENT TYPE: Book Chapter

Dennis, C.
Afro-colombian hip-hop: Globalization, popular music and ethnic identities
(2006) Studies in Latin American Popular Culture, (25), pp. 271-295.
LANGUAGE OF ORIGINAL DOCUMENT: English
DOCUMENT TYPE: Review

Hess, M.
Was Foucault a plagiarist? Hip-hop sampling and academic citation
(2006) Computers and Composition, 23 (3), pp. 280-295.
LANGUAGE OF ORIGINAL DOCUMENT: English
DOCUMENT TYPE: Article

Rice, J.
The making of ka-knowledge: Digital aurality
(2006) Computers and Composition, 23 (3), pp. 266-279.
LANGUAGE OF ORIGINAL DOCUMENT: English
DOCUMENT TYPE: Article

Rérat, P.
Rap in the steppes: The articulation between global and local processes in Mongolian hip-hop [Le rap des steppes l'articulation entre logiques globales et particularités locales dans le hip-hop mongol]
(2006) Geographie et Cultures, (59), pp. 43-55.
LANGUAGE OF ORIGINAL DOCUMENT: French
DOCUMENT TYPE: Article

Pereira, D., Sharma, S., Pichora-Fuller, K.
An acoustical study of IPOD output: Effects of headsets and control settings
(2006) Canadian Acoustics - Acoustique Canadienne, 34 (3), pp. 60-61.
LANGUAGE OF ORIGINAL DOCUMENT: English

DOCUMENT TYPE: Conference Paper

Blomquist, C.
Mash pit
(2006) Sportswear International, (208), pp. 144+146.
LANGUAGE OF ORIGINAL DOCUMENT: English
DOCUMENT TYPE: Article

Dagbovie, P.G.
Strategies for teaching African American history: Musings from the past, ruminations for the future
(2006) Journal of Negro Education, 75 (4), pp. 635-648.
LANGUAGE OF ORIGINAL DOCUMENT: English
DOCUMENT TYPE: Article

Collins, P.H.
New commodities, new consumers: Selling blackness in a global marketplace
(2006) Ethnicities, 6 (3), pp. 297-317.
LANGUAGE OF ORIGINAL DOCUMENT: English
DOCUMENT TYPE: Article

Worgs, D.C.
"Beware of the frustrated...": The fantasy and reality of African American violent revolt
(2006) Journal of Black Studies, 37 (1), pp. 20-45.
LANGUAGE OF ORIGINAL DOCUMENT: English
DOCUMENT TYPE: Article

Fallah, S., Pichora-Fuller, K.
An acoustical study of IPOD use by university students in quiet and noisy situations
(2006) Canadian Acoustics - Acoustique Canadienne, 34 (3), pp. 66-67.
LANGUAGE OF ORIGINAL DOCUMENT: English
DOCUMENT TYPE: Conference Paper

Alim, H.S.

Roc the mic right: The language of hip hop culture
(2006) Roc the Mic Right: The Language of Hip Hop Culture, pp. 1-184.
PUBLISHER: Routledge Taylor & Francis Group
LANGUAGE OF ORIGINAL DOCUMENT: English
DOCUMENT TYPE: Book

Kobin, C., Tyson, E.
Thematic analysis of hip-hop music: Can hip-hop in therapy facilitate empathic connections when working with clients in urban settings?
(2006) Arts in Psychotherapy, 33 (4), pp. 343-356.
LANGUAGE OF ORIGINAL DOCUMENT: English
DOCUMENT TYPE: Article

Balin-Brooks, T.L.
Wyclef Jean: Hip-hop mega-star works toward change in Haiti
(2006) Grassroots Development, 27 (1), pp. 36-37.
LANGUAGE OF ORIGINAL DOCUMENT: English
DOCUMENT TYPE: Article

De Grangeneuve, L.L.
Public action and hip-hop culture. The ambivalence of cultural political action [L'ambivalence des usages politiques de l'art: Action publique et culture hip-hop dans la métropole bordelaise]
(2006) Revue Francaise de Science Politique, 56 (3), pp. 457-477.
LANGUAGE OF ORIGINAL DOCUMENT: French
DOCUMENT TYPE: Article

Kalyan, R.
Hip-hop imaginaries: A genealogy of the present
(2006) Journal for Cultural Research, 10 (3), pp. 237-257.
LANGUAGE OF ORIGINAL DOCUMENT: English
DOCUMENT TYPE: Review

Jocson, K.M.
"Bob Dylan and Hip Hop": Intersecting literacy practices in youth poetry communities
(2006) Written Communication, 23 (3), pp. 231-259.

LANGUAGE OF ORIGINAL DOCUMENT: English
DOCUMENT TYPE: Article

Oliver, W.
"The Streets": An alternative black male socialization institution
(2006) Journal of Black Studies, 36 (6), pp. 918-937.
LANGUAGE OF ORIGINAL DOCUMENT: English

DOCUMENT TYPE: Article

Adams, T.M., Fuller, D.B.
The words have changed but the ideology remains the same misogynistic lyrics in rap music
(2006) Journal of Black Studies, 36 (6), pp. 938-957.
LANGUAGE OF ORIGINAL DOCUMENT: English
DOCUMENT TYPE: Review

Barrabés, E., Cors, J.M., Pinyol, C., Soler, J.
Hip-hop solutions of the 2N-body problem
(2006) Celestial Mechanics and Dynamical Astronomy, 95 (1-4), pp. 55-66.
LANGUAGE OF ORIGINAL DOCUMENT: English
DOCUMENT TYPE: Conference Paper

Omoniyi, T.

Hip-hop through the world Englishes lens: A response to globalization
(2006) World Englishes, 25 (2), pp. 195-208.
LANGUAGE OF ORIGINAL DOCUMENT: English
DOCUMENT TYPE: Article

Yeh, E.T., Lama, K.T.
Hip-hop gangsta or most deserving of victims? Transnational migrant identities and the paradox of Tibetan racialization in the USA
(2006) Environment and Planning A, 38 (5), pp. 809-829.
LANGUAGE OF ORIGINAL DOCUMENT: English
DOCUMENT TYPE: Review
ACCESS TYPE: Open Access

Leonard, D.J.
The real color of money: Controlling black bodies in the NBA
(2006) Journal of Sport and Social Issues, 30 (2), pp. 158-179.
LANGUAGE OF ORIGINAL DOCUMENT: English
DOCUMENT TYPE: Article

Lashua, B., Fox, K.
Rec needs a new rhythm cuz rap. Is where we're livin'
(2006) Leisure Sciences, 28 (3), pp. 267-283.
LANGUAGE OF ORIGINAL DOCUMENT: English
DOCUMENT TYPE: Article

Tanner-Smith, E.E., Williams, D.T., Nichols, D.
Selling sex to radio program directors: A content analysis of radio & records magazine
(2006) Sex Roles, 54 (9-10), pp. 675-686.
LANGUAGE OF ORIGINAL DOCUMENT: English
DOCUMENT TYPE: Article

Beckford, R.
Jesus dub: Theology, music and social change
(2006) Jesus Dub: Theology, Music and Social Change, pp. 1-182.
PUBLISHER: Routledge

LANGUAGE OF ORIGINAL DOCUMENT: English
DOCUMENT TYPE: Book

Niang, A.
Bboys: Hip-hop culture in Dakar, Sénégal
(2006) Global Youth?: Hybrid Identities, Plural Worlds, pp. 167-185.
PUBLISHER: Routledge Taylor & Francis Group
LANGUAGE OF ORIGINAL DOCUMENT: English
DOCUMENT TYPE: Book Chapter

Huq, R.
European youth cultures in a post-colonial world: British Asian underground and French hip-hop music scenes
(2006) Global Youth?: Hybrid Identities, Plural Worlds, pp. 14-31.
PUBLISHER: Routledge Taylor & Francis Group
LANGUAGE OF ORIGINAL DOCUMENT: English
DOCUMENT TYPE: Book Chapter

Arthur, D.
Authenticity and consumption in the Australian Hip Hop culture
(2006) Qualitative Market Research, 9 (2), pp. 140-156.
LANGUAGE OF ORIGINAL DOCUMENT: English
DOCUMENT TYPE: Article

Flores-González, N., Rodríguez, M., Rodríguez-Muñiz, M.
From hip-hop to humanization: Batey Urbano as a space for Latino youth culture and community action
(2006) Beyond Resistance!: Youth Activism and Community Change: New Democratic Possibilities for Practice and Policy for America's Youth, pp. 175-196.
PUBLISHER: Routledge Taylor & Francis Group
LANGUAGE OF ORIGINAL DOCUMENT: English
DOCUMENT TYPE: Book Chapter

Huq, R.
Beyond subculture: Pop, youth and identity in a postcolonial world
(2006) Beyond Subculture: Pop, Youth and Identity in a Postcolonial

World, pp. 1-217.
   PUBLISHER: Routledge Taylor & Francis Group
   LANGUAGE OF ORIGINAL DOCUMENT: English
   DOCUMENT TYPE: Book

Harrison Jr., L., Moore, L.N., Evans, L.
Ear to the streets: The race, hip-hop, and sports learning community at Louisiana State University
(2006) Journal of Black Studies, 36 (4), pp. 622-634.
LANGUAGE OF ORIGINAL DOCUMENT: English
DOCUMENT TYPE: Article

Ralph, M.
'Flirt[ing] with death' but 'still alive': The sexual dimension of surplus time in hip hop fantasy
(2006) Cultural Dynamics, 18 (1), pp. 61-88.
LANGUAGE OF ORIGINAL DOCUMENT: English
DOCUMENT TYPE: Article

Toynbee, J.
Copyright, the work and phonographic orality in music
(2006) Social and Legal Studies, 15 (1), pp. 77-99.
LANGUAGE OF ORIGINAL DOCUMENT: English
DOCUMENT TYPE: Article

Tyson, E.H.
Rap-music attitude and perception scale: A validation study
(2006) Research on Social Work Practice, 16 (2), pp. 211-223.
LANGUAGE OF ORIGINAL DOCUMENT: English
DOCUMENT TYPE: Article

Sanjek, D.
Ridiculing the 'White Bread Original': The politics of parody and preservation of greatness in Luther Campbell a.k.a. Luke Skywalker et al. v. Acuff-Rose Music, Inc
(2006) Cultural Studies, 20 (2-3), pp. 262-281.
LANGUAGE OF ORIGINAL DOCUMENT: English
DOCUMENT TYPE: Article

Hesmondhalgh, D.
Digital sampling and cultural inequality
(2006) Social and Legal Studies, 15 (1), pp. 53-75.
LANGUAGE OF ORIGINAL DOCUMENT: English
DOCUMENT TYPE: Article

Bailey, A.A.

A year in the life of the African-American male in advertising: A content analysis
(2006) Journal of Advertising, 35 (1), pp. 83-104.
LANGUAGE OF ORIGINAL DOCUMENT: English
DOCUMENT TYPE: Article

Smitherman, G.
Word from the mother: Language and African Americans
(2006) Word from the Mother: Language and African Americans, pp. 1-172.
    PUBLISHER: Routledge Taylor & Francis Group
    LANGUAGE OF ORIGINAL DOCUMENT: English
    DOCUMENT TYPE: Book

Lehr, J.C., Bartlett, J., Tabvahtah, J.
The distant beat of my father's drums: Contemporary Aboriginal music and NCI-FM broadcasting, Manitoba, Canada
(2006) GeoJournal, 65 (1-2), pp. 79-90.
    LANGUAGE OF ORIGINAL DOCUMENT: English
    DOCUMENT TYPE: Article

Covington-Ward, Y.
South Bronx Performances: The Reciprocal Relationship Between Hip-Hop and Black Girls' Musical Play
(2006) Women and Performance, 16 (1), pp. 119-134.
    LANGUAGE OF ORIGINAL DOCUMENT: English
    DOCUMENT TYPE: Article

Alim, H.S.
Re-inventing Islam with Unique Modern Tones: Muslim Hip Hop Artists as Verbal Mujahidin
(2006) Souls, 8 (4), pp. 45-58.
    LANGUAGE OF ORIGINAL DOCUMENT: English
    DOCUMENT TYPE: Article

O'Hanlon, R.
Australian hip hop: a sociolinguistic investigation
(2006) Australian Journal of Linguistics, 26 (2), pp. 193-209.
    LANGUAGE OF ORIGINAL DOCUMENT: English
    DOCUMENT TYPE: Article

Fitzgibbon, M.L., Stolley, M.R., Schiffer, L., Van Horn, L., KauferChristoffel, K., Dyer, A.
Hip-Hop to Health Jr. for Latino preschool children

(2006) Obesity, 14 (9), pp. 1616-1625.
PUBLISHER: Blackwell Publishing Inc.
LANGUAGE OF ORIGINAL DOCUMENT: English
DOCUMENT TYPE: Article
ACCESS TYPE: Open Access

Birchfield, D., West, M.L., Savenye, W., Rikakis, T.
Multimedia and hip-hop for experiential education
(2006) IEEE Signal Processing Magazine, 23 (4), pp. 10-13.
PUBLISHER: Institute of Electrical and Electronics Engineers Inc.
LANGUAGE OF ORIGINAL DOCUMENT: English
DOCUMENT TYPE: Article

Casco, J.A.S.
The Language of the Young People: Rap, Urban Culture and Protest in Tanzania
(2006) Journal of Asian and African Studies, 41 (3), pp. 229-248.
LANGUAGE OF ORIGINAL DOCUMENT: English
DOCUMENT TYPE: Article

Turner, R.B.
Constructing masculinity: Interactions between islam and african-american youth since C. Eric lincoln, the black muslims in america
(2006) Souls, 8 (4), pp. 31-44.
LANGUAGE OF ORIGINAL DOCUMENT: English
DOCUMENT TYPE: Article

Payne, Y.A.
"A gangster and a gentleman": how street life-oriented, U.S. - Born African men negotiate issues of survival in relation to their masculinity
(2006) Men and Masculinities, 8 (3), pp. 288-297.
LANGUAGE OF ORIGINAL DOCUMENT: English
DOCUMENT TYPE: Article

Reese, V.O.
Ready or Not: Lauryn Hill As Hip-Hop's Mammy: Wrighting HiSTORY: **The Per(form)ance of Absence through the SEXed and**

RACEd body of Harriet Jacobs in incidents in the Life of a Slave Girl
(2006) Women and Performance, 16 (1), pp. 157-166.
LANGUAGE OF ORIGINAL DOCUMENT: English
DOCUMENT TYPE: Article

Distiller, N.
'Petrarch's long-deceased woes'?: Petrarchism and hip-hop
(2006) Scrutiny2, 11 (1), pp. 46-64.
LANGUAGE OF ORIGINAL DOCUMENT: English
DOCUMENT TYPE: Article

Saucier, P.K.
Feminism and hip-hop conference, university of chicago (april 2005)
(2006) Journal of Popular Music Studies, 18 (1), pp. 94-101.
LANGUAGE OF ORIGINAL DOCUMENT: English
DOCUMENT TYPE: Article

Gaunt, K.D.
The games black girls play: Learning the ropes from double-dutch to hip-hop
(2006) The Games Black Girls Play: Learning the Ropes from Double-Dutch to Hip-Hop, pp. 1-220.
PUBLISHER: New York University Press
LANGUAGE OF ORIGINAL DOCUMENT: English
DOCUMENT TYPE: Book

Meineck, P.
Live from New York: Hip hop aeschylus and operatic aristophanes
(2006) Arion - Journal of Humanities and the Classics, 14 (1), pp. 145-167.
PUBLISHER: Boston University Arion
LANGUAGE OF ORIGINAL DOCUMENT: English
DOCUMENT TYPE: Review

Alim, H.S.
"The natti ain't no punk city": Emic views of Hip Hop cultures

(2006) Callaloo, 29 (3), pp. 969-990.
PUBLISHER: Johns Hopkins University Press
LANGUAGE OF ORIGINAL DOCUMENT: English
DOCUMENT TYPE: Review

Heath, R.S.
Hip-hop now: An introduction
(2006) Callaloo, 29 (3), pp. 714-716.
PUBLISHER: Johns Hopkins University Press
LANGUAGE OF ORIGINAL DOCUMENT: English
DOCUMENT TYPE: Editorial

Spady, J.G.
The fluoroscope of Brooklyn Hip Hop: Talib Kweli in conversation
(2006) Callaloo, 29 (3), pp. 993-1011.

PUBLISHER: Johns Hopkins University Press
LANGUAGE OF ORIGINAL DOCUMENT: English
DOCUMENT TYPE: Review

Heath, R.S.
True heads: Historicizing the hip-hop "nation" in context
(2006) Callaloo, 29 (3), pp. 846-866.
PUBLISHER: Johns Hopkins University Press
LANGUAGE OF ORIGINAL DOCUMENT: English
DOCUMENT TYPE: Review

Marshall, W.
Giving up hip-hop's firstborn: A quest for the real after the death of sampling
(2006) Callaloo, 29 (3), pp. 868-892.
PUBLISHER: Johns Hopkins University Press
LANGUAGE OF ORIGINAL DOCUMENT: English
DOCUMENT TYPE: Review

Peterson, J.
"Dead prezence": Money and mortal themes in hip hop culture
(2006) Callaloo, 29 (3), pp. 895-909.
PUBLISHER: Johns Hopkins University Press
LANGUAGE OF ORIGINAL DOCUMENT: English
DOCUMENT TYPE: Review

Pavlic, E.
Rap, soul, and the vortex at 33.3 RPM: Hip-hop's implements and African American modernisms
(2006) Callaloo, 29 (3), pp. 956-968.
PUBLISHER: Johns Hopkins University Press
LANGUAGE OF ORIGINAL DOCUMENT: English
DOCUMENT TYPE: Review

Norman, B.
The politics of Austrian hip-hop: HC Strache's xenophobia gets dissed
(2006) Colloquia Germanica, 39 (2), pp. 209-230.

PUBLISHER: A. Francke Verlag GmbH
LANGUAGE OF ORIGINAL DOCUMENT: English
DOCUMENT TYPE: Review

Sarkar, M., Winer, L.
Multilingual codeswitching in quebec rap: Poetry, pragmatics and performativity
(2006) International Journal of Multilingualism, 3 (3), pp. 173-192.
LANGUAGE OF ORIGINAL DOCUMENT: English
DOCUMENT TYPE: Article

Haupt, A.
Race, Audience, Multitude: Afrikaans Arts Festivals and the Politics of Inclusion
(2006) Muziki, 3 (1), pp. 16-27.
LANGUAGE OF ORIGINAL DOCUMENT: English
DOCUMENT TYPE: Article

Segalo, P.
The psychological power of rap music in the healing of black communities
(2006) Muziki, 3 (1), pp. 28-35.
LANGUAGE OF ORIGINAL DOCUMENT: English
DOCUMENT TYPE: Article

Chatterjee, S.
Impossible Hosting: D'lo Sets an Undomesticated Stage for South Asian Youth Artists
(2006) Women and Performance, 16 (3), pp. 443-462.
LANGUAGE OF ORIGINAL DOCUMENT: English
DOCUMENT TYPE: Article

Raphael-Hernandez, H., Steen, S.
AfroAsian encounters: Culture, history, politics
(2006) AfroAsian Encounters: Culture, History, Politics, pp. 1-342.
PUBLISHER: New York University Press
LANGUAGE OF ORIGINAL DOCUMENT: English
DOCUMENT TYPE: Book

Wood, A.
'New forms': Towards a critical dialogue with black British 'popular' fictions
(2006) A Black British Canon?, pp. 105-125.
PUBLISHER: Palgrave Macmillan
LANGUAGE OF ORIGINAL DOCUMENT: English
DOCUMENT TYPE: Book Chapter

Chenciner, A.
Symmetries and "simple" solutions of the classical n-body problem
(2006) XIVth International Congress on Mathematical Physics: Lisbon, 28 July - 2 August 2003, pp. 4-20.
PUBLISHER: World Scientific Publishing Co.
LANGUAGE OF ORIGINAL DOCUMENT: English
DOCUMENT TYPE: Book Chapter

Harris, K.
Boys, boyz, bois: An ethics of Black masculinity in film and popular media
(2005) Boys, Boyz, Bois: An Ethics of Black Masculinity in Film and Popular Media, pp. 1-156.
PUBLISHER: Routledge
LANGUAGE OF ORIGINAL DOCUMENT: English
DOCUMENT TYPE: Book

Case, E.
This is London speaking
(2005) New Scientist, 188 (2528), pp. 50-51.
LANGUAGE OF ORIGINAL DOCUMENT: English
DOCUMENT TYPE: Review

Hess, M.
Hip-hop realness and the white performer
(2005) Critical Studies in Media Communication, 22 (5), pp. 372-389.
LANGUAGE OF ORIGINAL DOCUMENT: English
DOCUMENT TYPE: Review

Solomon, T.
'Living underground is tough': Authenticity and locality in the hip-hop community in Istanbul, Turkey
(2005) Popular Music, 24 (1), pp. 1-20.
LANGUAGE OF ORIGINAL DOCUMENT: English
DOCUMENT TYPE: Review

Fleetwood, N.R.
Hip-hop fashion, masculine anxiety, and the discourse of Americana
(2005) Black Cultural Traffic: Crossroads in Global Performance and

Popular Culture, pp. 326-345.
  PUBLISHER: University of Michigan Press
  LANGUAGE OF ORIGINAL DOCUMENT: English
  DOCUMENT TYPE: Book Chapter

Hoyler, M., Mager, C.
Hiphop ist im Haus: Cultural policy, community centres, and the making of hip-hop music in Germany
(2005) Built Environment, 31 (3), pp. 237-250.
LANGUAGE OF ORIGINAL DOCUMENT: English
DOCUMENT TYPE: Article

Hess, M.
Metal faces, rap masks: Identity and resistance in hip hop's persona artist
(2005) Popular Music and Society, 28 (3), pp. 297-311.
LANGUAGE OF ORIGINAL DOCUMENT: English
DOCUMENT TYPE: Article

Osumare, H.
Global hip-hop and the African diaspora
(2005) Black Cultural Traffic: Crossroads in Global Performance and Popular Culture, pp. 266-288.
PUBLISHER: University of Michigan Press
LANGUAGE OF ORIGINAL DOCUMENT: English
DOCUMENT TYPE: Book Chapter

Stroeken, K.
Immunizing strategies: Hip-hop and critique in Tanzania
(2005) Africa, 75 (4), pp. 488-509.
LANGUAGE OF ORIGINAL DOCUMENT: English
DOCUMENT TYPE: Article

Fink, R.
The story of ORCH5, or, the classical ghost in the hip-hop machine
(2005) Popular Music, 24 (3), pp. 339-356.
LANGUAGE OF ORIGINAL DOCUMENT: English
DOCUMENT TYPE: Review

Monaghan, T.

Breakin' convention 05 - International festival of hip hop dance theatre
(2005) Dancing Times, 95 (1139), .
LANGUAGE OF ORIGINAL DOCUMENT: English
DOCUMENT TYPE: Article

The masculine finery of Louis XIV: With hip hop [La parure masculine de Louis XIV: Au hip hop]
(2005) Oeil, (576), pp. 59-61.
LANGUAGE OF ORIGINAL DOCUMENT: French
DOCUMENT TYPE: Note

Crossley, S.
Metaphorical conceptions in hip-hop music
(2005) African American Review, 39 (4), pp. 501-512.
LANGUAGE OF ORIGINAL DOCUMENT: English
DOCUMENT TYPE: Article

Monaghan, T.
Hip hop legends at the South Bank
(2005) Dancing Times, 95 (1137), pp. 45-46.
LANGUAGE OF ORIGINAL DOCUMENT: English
DOCUMENT TYPE: Article

Baker, G.
!Hip hop, revolución! Nationalizing rap in Cuba
(2005) Ethnomusicology, 49 (3), pp. 368-402.
LANGUAGE OF ORIGINAL DOCUMENT: English
DOCUMENT TYPE: Article

Morgan, M.
Hip-hop women shredding the veil: Race and class in popular feminist identity
(2005) South Atlantic Quarterly, 104 (3), pp. 425-444.
LANGUAGE OF ORIGINAL DOCUMENT: English
DOCUMENT TYPE: Review

Stephens, V.
Pop goes the rapper: A close reading of Eminem's genderphobia
(2005) Popular Music, 24 (1), pp. 21-36.
LANGUAGE OF ORIGINAL DOCUMENT: English
DOCUMENT TYPE: Review

Hess, M.
"Don't Quote Me, Boy": Dynamite Hack covers NWA's "boyz-N-The-Hood"
(2005) Popular Music and Society, 28 (2), pp. 179-191.
LANGUAGE OF ORIGINAL DOCUMENT: English
DOCUMENT TYPE: Article

Sernoe, J.
"Now we're on the top, top of the pops": The performance of "non-Mainstream" music on Billboard's albums charts, 1981-2001
(2005) Popular Music and Society, 28 (5), pp. 639-662.
LANGUAGE OF ORIGINAL DOCUMENT: English
DOCUMENT TYPE: Review

Wallach, J.
Engineering techno-hybrid grooves in two Indonesian sound studios
(2005) Wired for Sound: Engineering and Technologies in Sonic Cultures, pp. 138-155.
PUBLISHER: Wesleyan University Press
LANGUAGE OF ORIGINAL DOCUMENT: English
DOCUMENT TYPE: Book Chapter

Ouassini, A.
WHAT'S HAPPENING TO S.I.: G. FINE
(2005) Studies in Symbolic Interaction, 28, pp. 355-361.
EDITORS: Hirschey M., John K., Makhija A.K.
LANGUAGE OF ORIGINAL DOCUMENT: English
DOCUMENT TYPE: Review

Tyson, E.H.
The rap music attitude and perception (RAP) scale: Scale

development and preliminary analysis of psychometric properties

(2005) Journal of Human Behavior in the Social Environment, 11 (3-4), pp. 59-82.

LANGUAGE OF ORIGINAL DOCUMENT: English

DOCUMENT TYPE: Review

Berens, R.S.
Another "new" metric for outdoor amphitheater criteria
(2005) 19th National Conference on Noise Control Engineering 2005, Noise-Con 05, 1, pp. 227-234.
CONFERENCE NAME: 19th National Conference on Noise Control Engineering 2005, Noise-Con 2005
CONFERENCE DATE: 15 October 2005 through 17 October 2005
CONFERENCE LOCATION: Minneapolis, MN
LANGUAGE OF ORIGINAL DOCUMENT: English
DOCUMENT TYPE: Conference Paper

Porcello, T.
Music mediated as live in Austin: Sound, technology, and recording practice
(2005) Wired for Sound: Engineering and Technologies in Sonic Cultures, pp. 103-117.
PUBLISHER: Wesleyan University Press
LANGUAGE OF ORIGINAL DOCUMENT: English
DOCUMENT TYPE: Book Chapter

Lee, V.
Smarts: A cautionary tale
(2005) Calling Cards: Theory and Practice in The Study of Race, Gender, and Culture, pp. 93-105.
PUBLISHER: State University of New York Press
LANGUAGE OF ORIGINAL DOCUMENT: English
DOCUMENT TYPE: Book Chapter

Kun, J.
Audiotopia: Music, race, and America
(2005) Audiotopia: Music, Race, and America, pp. 1-302.
PUBLISHER: University of California Press
LANGUAGE OF ORIGINAL DOCUMENT: English
DOCUMENT TYPE: Book

Calhoun, L.R.

"Will the real slim shady please stand up?: Masking whiteness, encoding hegemonic masculinity in Eminem's Marshall Mathers LP
(2005) Howard Journal of Communications, 16 (4), pp. 267-294.
LANGUAGE OF ORIGINAL DOCUMENT: English
DOCUMENT TYPE: Review

Riley, A.
The rebirth of tragedy out of the spirit of hip hop: A cultural sociology of gangsta rap music
(2005) Journal of Youth Studies, 8 (3), pp. 297-311.
LANGUAGE OF ORIGINAL DOCUMENT: English
DOCUMENT TYPE: Review

Maher, G.C.
Brechtian hip-hop didactics and self-production in post-gangsta political mixtapes
(2005) Journal of Black Studies, 36 (1), pp. 129-160.
LANGUAGE OF ORIGINAL DOCUMENT: English
DOCUMENT TYPE: Article

Watts, E.K.
Border patrolling and "passing" in Eminem's 8 mile
(2005) Critical Studies in Media Communication, 22 (3), pp. 187-206.
LANGUAGE OF ORIGINAL DOCUMENT: English
DOCUMENT TYPE: Review

Trapp, E.
The push and pull of hip-hop: A social movement analysis
(2005) American Behavioral Scientist, 48 (11), pp. 1482-1495.
LANGUAGE OF ORIGINAL DOCUMENT: English
DOCUMENT TYPE: Conference Paper

Perullo, A.
Hooligans and heroes: Youth identity and hip-hop in Dar es Salaam, Tanzania
(2005) Africa Today, 51 (4), pp. 75-101.
LANGUAGE OF ORIGINAL DOCUMENT: English
DOCUMENT TYPE: Article

Au, W.
Fresh out of school: Rap music's discursive battle with education
(2005) Journal of Negro Education, 74 (3), pp. 210-220.
LANGUAGE OF ORIGINAL DOCUMENT: English
DOCUMENT TYPE: Article

Holme, P., Grönlund, A.
Modelling the dynamics of youth subcultures
(2005) JASSS, 8 (3), 12 p.
LANGUAGE OF ORIGINAL DOCUMENT: English
DOCUMENT TYPE: Article

De Freitas, E.
Pre-Service Teachers and the Reinscription of Whiteness: Disrupting dominant cultural codes through textual analysis
(2005) Teaching Education, 16 (2), pp. 151-164.
LANGUAGE OF ORIGINAL DOCUMENT: English
DOCUMENT TYPE: Review

Scott, J.
A new aesthetics of black equality: On Tony Medina
(2005) Race and Class, 46 (4), pp. 20-38.
LANGUAGE OF ORIGINAL DOCUMENT: English
DOCUMENT TYPE: Article

Hagedorn, J.M.
The global impact of gangs
(2005) Journal of Contemporary Criminal Justice, 21 (2), pp. 153-169.
LANGUAGE OF ORIGINAL DOCUMENT: English
DOCUMENT TYPE: Article

Hutnyk, J.
The dialectics of european hip-hop
(2005) South Asian Popular Culture, 3 (1), pp. 17-32.
LANGUAGE OF ORIGINAL DOCUMENT: English
DOCUMENT TYPE: Article

Youngquist, P.
The Afro Futurism of DJ Vassa
(2005) European Romantic Review, 16 (2), pp. 181-192.
LANGUAGE OF ORIGINAL DOCUMENT: English
DOCUMENT TYPE: Article

Stephens, D.P., Phillips, L.
Integrating Black feminist thought into conceptual frameworks of African American adolescent women's sexual scripting processes
(2005) Sexualities, Evolution and Gender, 7 (1), pp. 37-55.
LANGUAGE OF ORIGINAL DOCUMENT: English
DOCUMENT TYPE: Review

Kosminsky, E.V., Daniel, L.
TOYS AND GAMES: CHILDHOOD IN THE PARQUE DAS NAÇÕES FAVELA IN BRAZIL
(2005) Sociological Studies of Children and Youth, 10, pp. 23-41.
EDITORS: Bass L.
LANGUAGE OF ORIGINAL DOCUMENT: English
DOCUMENT TYPE: Review

Kun, J.
Audiotopia: Music, race, and America
(2005) Audiotopia: Music, Race, and America, 302 p.
PUBLISHER: University of California Press
LANGUAGE OF ORIGINAL DOCUMENT: English
DOCUMENT TYPE: Book

Fitzgibbon, M.L., Stolley, M.R., Schiffer, L., Van Horn, L., Kauferchristoffel, K., Dyer, A.
Two-year follow-up results for Hip-Hop to Health Jr.: A randomized controlled trial for overweight prevention in preschool minority children
(2005) Journal of Pediatrics, 146 (5), pp. 618-625.
PUBLISHER: Mosby Inc.
LANGUAGE OF ORIGINAL DOCUMENT: English
DOCUMENT TYPE: Article

Scott, J.
Dynamic multiculturalism: A race-free concept of America
(2005) Rethinking Marxism, 17 (1), pp. 139-145.
LANGUAGE OF ORIGINAL DOCUMENT: English
DOCUMENT TYPE: Article

Steingo, G.
Guthrie P. Ramsey, Jr. race music: Black cultures from bebop to hip-hop. berkeley, los angeles, and london: University of california press, 2003. xii, 281 pp., isbn 0-520-21048-4, no. 7 in music of the african diaspora, a series edited by samuel A. Floyd, Jr.
(2005) Muziki, 2 (1), pp. 61-65.
LANGUAGE OF ORIGINAL DOCUMENT: English
DOCUMENT TYPE: Article

Ferrell, J., Greer, C., Jewkes, Y.
Hip hop graffiti, Mexican murals and the war on terror
(2005) Crime Media Culture, 1 (1), pp. 5-9.
LANGUAGE OF ORIGINAL DOCUMENT: English
DOCUMENT TYPE: Editorial
ACCESS TYPE: Open Access

Geidel, M.
Supermaxes, stripmines, and hip-hop
(2005) Journal of Popular Music Studies, 17 (1), pp. 67-76.
LANGUAGE OF ORIGINAL DOCUMENT: English
DOCUMENT TYPE: Article

Gordon, L.R.
The problem of maturity in hip hop
(2005) Review of Education, Pedagogy, and Cultural Studies, 27 (4), pp. 367-389.
LANGUAGE OF ORIGINAL DOCUMENT: English
DOCUMENT TYPE: Article

Newman, M.
Rap as literacy: A genre analysis of Hip-Hop ciphers
(2005) Text, 25 (3), pp. 399-436.
PUBLISHER: De Gruyter Mouton
LANGUAGE OF ORIGINAL DOCUMENT: English
DOCUMENT TYPE: Article

Cheney, C.
Brothers Gonna Work It Out: Sexual politics in the golden age of rap nationalism
(2005) Brothers Gonna Work It Out: Sexual Politics in the Golden Age of Rap Nationalism, pp. 1-221.
PUBLISHER: New York University Press
LANGUAGE OF ORIGINAL DOCUMENT: English
DOCUMENT TYPE: Book

DeBose, C.
The sociology of African American language: A language planning perspective
(2005) The Sociology of African American Language: A Language Planning Perspective, pp. 1-237.
PUBLISHER: Palgrave Macmillan
LANGUAGE OF ORIGINAL DOCUMENT: English
DOCUMENT TYPE: Book

Davis, J.E.
Black boys at school: Negotiating masculinities and race
(2005) Educating Our Black Children: New Directions and Radical Approaches, pp. 169-182.
PUBLISHER: Taylor and Francis
LANGUAGE OF ORIGINAL DOCUMENT: English
DOCUMENT TYPE: Book Chapter

Dlamini, S.N.
Youth and identity politics in South Africa, 1990–1994
(2005) Youth and Identity Politics in South Africa, 1990-94, pp. 1-233.
PUBLISHER: University of Toronto Press
LANGUAGE OF ORIGINAL DOCUMENT: English
DOCUMENT TYPE: Book

Gormley, P.
The new-brutality film race and affect in contemporary hollywood cinema
(2005) The New-Brutality Film Race and Affect in Contemporary Hollywood Cinema, pp. 1-221.
PUBLISHER: Intellect Ltd.
LANGUAGE OF ORIGINAL DOCUMENT: English
DOCUMENT TYPE: Book

Cook, S.E.
New technologies and language change: Toward an anthropology of linguistic frontiers
(2004) Annual Review of Anthropology, 33, pp. 103-115.
LANGUAGE OF ORIGINAL DOCUMENT: English
DOCUMENT TYPE: Article

Sylvia, F.
Filles et garçons en danse hip-hop la production institutionnelle de pratiques sexuées
(2004) Societes Contemporaines, 55 (3), pp. 5-20.
LANGUAGE OF ORIGINAL DOCUMENT: French
DOCUMENT TYPE: Article

Kitwana, B.
The state of the hip-hop generation: How hip-hop's cultural movement is evolving into political power
(2004) Diogenes, 51 (3), pp. 115-120.
LANGUAGE OF ORIGINAL DOCUMENT: English
DOCUMENT TYPE: Article

Sommer, S.
Prophets in pumas: When hip hop broke out
(2004) Dance Magazine, 78 (7), p. 30.
LANGUAGE OF ORIGINAL DOCUMENT: English
DOCUMENT TYPE: Article

Murray, D.C.
Hip-hop vs. high art: Notes on race as spectacle
(2004) Art Journal, 63 (2), pp. 5-19.
LANGUAGE OF ORIGINAL DOCUMENT: English

DOCUMENT TYPE: Article

Condry, I.
B-Boys and b-girls: Rap fandom and consumer culture in Japan
(2004) Fanning the Flames: Fans and Consumer Culture in Contemporary Japan, pp. 17-39.
PUBLISHER: State University of New York Press
LANGUAGE OF ORIGINAL DOCUMENT: English
DOCUMENT TYPE: Book Chapter

Kohn, N., Lee, Y.S.
Musikonceit: A postmodern Bravura Sans footnotes
(2004) Cultural Studies - Critical Methodologies, 4 (1), pp. 112-127.
LANGUAGE OF ORIGINAL DOCUMENT: English
DOCUMENT TYPE: Article

Mori, H., Ohta, S., Hoshino, J.
Automatic dance generation from music annotation
(2004) ACM International Conference Proceeding Series, 74, pp. 352-353.
CONFERENCE NAME: ACM SIGCHI International Conference on Advances in Computer Entertainment Technology, ACE 2004
CONFERENCE DATE: 3 June 2005 through 5 June 2005
CONFERENCE LOCATION: Singapore
LANGUAGE OF ORIGINAL DOCUMENT: English
DOCUMENT TYPE: Conference Paper

Selfe, C.L.
Students who teach us: A case study of a new media text designer
(2004) Writing new media: Theory and applications for expanding the teaching of composition, pp. 43-66.
PUBLISHER: Utah State University Press
LANGUAGE OF ORIGINAL DOCUMENT: English
DOCUMENT TYPE: Book Chapter

Kim, J., Singer, R.N., Chung, S., Lee, A., Moon, D., Kim, W.
Mood alteration related to aerobic, anaerobic and rhythmic exercises

(2004) Journal of Human Movement Studies, 47 (2), pp. 105-117.
LANGUAGE OF ORIGINAL DOCUMENT: English
DOCUMENT TYPE: Article

Kern, J.
Hip hop and french songs [Hip Hop und französische Chansons]
(2004) TextilWirtschaft, (44), pp. 74-75.
LANGUAGE OF ORIGINAL DOCUMENT: German
DOCUMENT TYPE: Note

Beachum, F.D., McCray, C.R.
Cultural collision in urban schools
(2004) Current Issues in Education, 7, .
LANGUAGE OF ORIGINAL DOCUMENT: English
DOCUMENT TYPE: Review

Stokes, M.
Ethnicity, identity and the global city [Musique, identité et "ville-monde": Perspectives critiques]
(2004) Homme, (171-172), pp. 371-388.
LANGUAGE OF ORIGINAL DOCUMENT: French
DOCUMENT TYPE: Review

Piekarski, B.
The rap on hip-hop
(2004) Library Journal, 129 (12), pp. 47-50.
LANGUAGE OF ORIGINAL DOCUMENT: English
DOCUMENT TYPE: Review

Funk, O.F., Kettmann, V., Drimal, J., Langer, T.
Chemical function based pharmacophore generation of endothelin-A selective receptor antagonists
(2004) Journal of Medicinal Chemistry, 47 (11), pp. 2750-2760.
LANGUAGE OF ORIGINAL DOCUMENT: English
DOCUMENT TYPE: Article

Ragaller, S.

Kids are buying bright colours. At last! [Die kids kaufen knall-farben. Endlich!]
(2004) TextilWirtschaft, (17), pp. 74-75.
LANGUAGE OF ORIGINAL DOCUMENT: German
DOCUMENT TYPE: Article

Butler, P.
Much respect: Toward a hip-hop theory of punishment
(2004) Stanford Law Review, 56 (5), pp. 983-1016.
LANGUAGE OF ORIGINAL DOCUMENT: English
DOCUMENT TYPE: Conference Paper

Miranda, D., Claes, M.
Rap music genres and deviant behaviors in French-Canadian adolescents
(2004) Journal of Youth and Adolescence, 33 (2), pp. 113-122.
LANGUAGE OF ORIGINAL DOCUMENT: English
DOCUMENT TYPE: Article

Pardue, D.
"Writing in the margins": Brazilian hip-hop as an educational project
(2004) Anthropology and Education Quarterly, 35 (4), pp. 411-432.
PUBLISHER: Wiley-Blackwell
LANGUAGE OF ORIGINAL DOCUMENT: English
DOCUMENT TYPE: Article

Alim, H.S.
Hip hop nation language
(2004) Language in the USA: Themes for the Twenty-First Century, pp. 387-409.
PUBLISHER: Cambridge University Press
LANGUAGE OF ORIGINAL DOCUMENT: English
DOCUMENT TYPE: Book Chapter

Faure, S.
Institutionnalisation de la danse hip-hop et récits autobiographiques des artistes chorégraphes

(2004) Geneses, 55 (2), pp. 84-106.
PUBLISHER: Editions Belin

LANGUAGE OF ORIGINAL DOCUMENT: French
DOCUMENT TYPE: Article

Snapper, J.
Scratching the Surface: Spinning Time and Identity in Hip-Hop Turntablism
(2004) European Journal of Cultural Studies, 7 (1), pp. 9-25.
LANGUAGE OF ORIGINAL DOCUMENT: English
DOCUMENT TYPE: Article

Adejunmobi, M.
Polyglots, vernaculars and global markets: Variable trends in west africa
(2004) Language and Intercultural Communication, 4 (3), pp. 159-174.
LANGUAGE OF ORIGINAL DOCUMENT: English
DOCUMENT TYPE: Article

Neal, M.A.
Up from hustling: Power, plantations, and the hip–hop mogul
(2004) International Journal of Phytoremediation, 21 (1), pp. 157-182.
LANGUAGE OF ORIGINAL DOCUMENT: English
DOCUMENT TYPE: Article

Morgan, M.
Preserving hip hop culture
(2004) International Journal of Phytoremediation, 21 (1), pp. 207-214.
LANGUAGE OF ORIGINAL DOCUMENT: English
DOCUMENT TYPE: Article

Aidi, H.
"Verily, there is only one hip–hop umma": Islam, cultural protest and urban marginality
(2004) International Journal of Phytoremediation, 21 (1), pp. 107-126.
LANGUAGE OF ORIGINAL DOCUMENT: English
DOCUMENT TYPE: Article

Mu'id, N.
Live, from newark: The national hip hop political convention
(2004) International Journal of Phytoremediation, 21 (1), pp. 221-229.
LANGUAGE OF ORIGINAL DOCUMENT: English
DOCUMENT TYPE: Article

Naison, M.
From doo wop to hip hop: The bittersweet odyssey of african–americans in the south bronx
(2004) International Journal of Phytoremediation, 21 (1), pp. 37-49.
LANGUAGE OF ORIGINAL DOCUMENT: English
DOCUMENT TYPE: Article

Kitwana, B.
Hip–hop studies and the new culture wars
(2004) International Journal of Phytoremediation, 21 (1), pp. 73-77.
LANGUAGE OF ORIGINAL DOCUMENT: English
DOCUMENT TYPE: Article

Powell, K.
The hip–hop generation
(2004) International Journal of Phytoremediation, 21 (1), pp. 7-8.
LANGUAGE OF ORIGINAL DOCUMENT: English
DOCUMENT TYPE: Article

Ford, R.

Hip–hop white wash: The impact of eminem on rap music and music industry economics

(2004) International Journal of Phytoremediation, 21 (1), pp. 127-134.
LANGUAGE OF ORIGINAL DOCUMENT: English
DOCUMENT TYPE: Article

Boyd, T.

Inter generational culture wars: Civil rights vs hip hop

(2004) International Journal of Phytoremediation, 21 (1), pp. 51-69.
LANGUAGE OF ORIGINAL DOCUMENT: English
DOCUMENT TYPE: Article

Baker, R.

"Take me to your leader": A critical analysis of the hip–hop summit action network

(2004) International Journal of Phytoremediation, 21 (1), pp. 215-219.
LANGUAGE OF ORIGINAL DOCUMENT: English
DOCUMENT TYPE: Article

Nuruddin, Y.

Brothas gonna work it out! hip hop philanthropy, black power vision, and the future of the race: The new hnic and the new hbcus: Inter generational collaboration, internal reparations, and the establishment of communiversity leadership academies

(2004) International Journal of Phytoremediation, 21 (1), pp. 231-304.
LANGUAGE OF ORIGINAL DOCUMENT: English
DOCUMENT TYPE: Article

Wright, K.

Rise up hip hop nation: From deconstructing racial politics to building positive solutions

(2004) International Journal of Phytoremediation, 21 (1), pp. 9-20.
LANGUAGE OF ORIGINAL DOCUMENT: English
DOCUMENT TYPE: Article

Martinez, G.
The politics of hip hop
(2004) International Journal of Phytoremediation, 21 (1), pp. 195-205.
LANGUAGE OF ORIGINAL DOCUMENT: English
DOCUMENT TYPE: Article

Nyairo, J.
'Reading the referents': The ghost of America in contemporary Kenyan popular music
(2004) Scrutiny2, 9 (1), pp. 39-55.
LANGUAGE OF ORIGINAL DOCUMENT: English
DOCUMENT TYPE: Article

Tyson, E.H.
Rap music in social work practice with african-americanand latino youth: A conceptual model with practical applications
(2004) Journal of Human Behavior in the Social Environment, 8 (4), pp. 1-21.
LANGUAGE OF ORIGINAL DOCUMENT: English
DOCUMENT TYPE: Article

King, C.R.
Apologies and apologists: The disavowal of racism and the abjuration of anti-racism in the contemporary United States
(2004) SIMILE, 4 (4), art. no. 54, .
PUBLISHER: University of Toronto Press
LANGUAGE OF ORIGINAL DOCUMENT: English
DOCUMENT TYPE: Review

Demers, J.
Sampling the 1970s in hip-hop
(2003) Popular Music, 22 (1), pp. 41-56.
LANGUAGE OF ORIGINAL DOCUMENT: English
DOCUMENT TYPE: Article

Smith-Shomade, B.E.
"Rock-a-bye, baby!": Black women disrupting gangs and constructing hip-hop gangsta films

(2003) Cinema Journal, 42 (2), pp. 25-40.
LANGUAGE OF ORIGINAL DOCUMENT: English

DOCUMENT TYPE: Review

Quintero, S.
One love : Transcommunality among the hip hop generation
(2003) Transcommunality: From The Politics of Conversion to the Ethics of Respect, pp. 211-218.
PUBLISHER: Temple University Press
LANGUAGE OF ORIGINAL DOCUMENT: English
DOCUMENT TYPE: Book Chapter

Johnson, L.A.
The spirit is willing and so is the flesh: The queen in hip-hop culture
(2003) Noise and Spirit: The Religious and Spiritual Sensibilities of Rap Music, pp. 154-170.
PUBLISHER: NYU Press
LANGUAGE OF ORIGINAL DOCUMENT: English
DOCUMENT TYPE: Book Chapter

Floyd-Thomas, J.M.
A jihad of words: The evolution of African American Islam and contemporary hip-hop
(2003) Noise and Spirit: The Religious and Spiritual Sensibilities of Rap Music, pp. 49-70.
PUBLISHER: NYU Press
LANGUAGE OF ORIGINAL DOCUMENT: English
DOCUMENT TYPE: Book Chapter

A., R.
I am naked underneath: The hip-hop gives the color [Je suis toute nue en dessous: Le hip-hop donne la couleur]
(2003) Oeil, (549), p. 171.
LANGUAGE OF ORIGINAL DOCUMENT: French
DOCUMENT TYPE: Short Survey

Aidi, H.
Let us be Moors: Islam, race and "connected histories"
(2003) Middle East Report, (229), pp. 42-53.
LANGUAGE OF ORIGINAL DOCUMENT: English
DOCUMENT TYPE: Article

Felton, C., Wang, C.-J.
Intelligent music classification with support vector machines
(2003) Intelligent Engineering Systems Through Artificial Neural Networks, 13, pp. 963-968.
EDITORS: Dagli C.H., Buczak A.L., Ghosh J., Embrechts M., Ersoy O.
SPONSORS: American Society of Mechanical Engineers, ASME
CONFERENCE NAME: Smart Engineering System Design: Neural Networks, Fuzzy Logic, Evolutionary Programming, Complex Systems and Artificial Life - Proceedings of the Artificial Neural Networks in Engineering Conference
CONFERENCE DATE: 2 November 2003 through 5 November 2003
CONFERENCE LOCATION: St. Louis, MO.
LANGUAGE OF ORIGINAL DOCUMENT: English
DOCUMENT TYPE: Conference Paper

Sullivan, R.E.

Rap and race: It's got a nice beat, but what about the message?
(2003) Journal of Black Studies, 33 (5), pp. 605-622.
LANGUAGE OF ORIGINAL DOCUMENT: English
DOCUMENT TYPE: Review

Fischer, P.D.
Challenging music as expression in the united states
(2003) Policing Pop, pp. 221-237.
PUBLISHER: Temple University Press
LANGUAGE OF ORIGINAL DOCUMENT: English
DOCUMENT TYPE: Book Chapter

El-Tayeb, F.
**'If you can't pronounce my name, you can just call me pride':
Afro-German activism, gender and hip hop**
(2003) Gender and History, 15 (3), pp. 460-486.
LANGUAGE OF ORIGINAL DOCUMENT: English
DOCUMENT TYPE: Article

Mattar, Y.
**Virtual communities and hip-hop music consumers in Singapore:
Interplaying global, local and subcultural identities**
(2003) Leisure Studies, 22 (4), pp. 283-300.
LANGUAGE OF ORIGINAL DOCUMENT: English
DOCUMENT TYPE: Article

Condoms go hip-hop.
(2003) AIDS patient care and STDs, 17 (10), pp. 545-546.
LANGUAGE OF ORIGINAL DOCUMENT: English
DOCUMENT TYPE: Article

Fernandes, S.
**Fear of a Black Nation: Local Rappers, Transnational Crossings,
and State Power in Contemporary Cuba**
(2003) Anthropological Quarterly, 76 (4), pp. 575-608.
LANGUAGE OF ORIGINAL DOCUMENT: English
DOCUMENT TYPE: Review

Stallings, L.H.
"I'm goin pimp whores!" The goines factor and the theory of a hip-hop neo-slave narrative
(2003) New Centennial Review, 3 (3), pp. 175-203.
LANGUAGE OF ORIGINAL DOCUMENT: English
DOCUMENT TYPE: Review

Clay, A.
Keepin' it real: Black youth, hip-hop culture, and black identity
(2003) American Behavioral Scientist, 46 (10), pp. 1346-1358.
LANGUAGE OF ORIGINAL DOCUMENT: English
DOCUMENT TYPE: Conference Paper

Ramsey, G.P., Jr.
Race Music: Black Cultures from Bebop to Hip-Hop
(2003) Race Music: Black Cultures from Bebop to Hip-Hop, pp. 1-281.
PUBLISHER: University of California Press
LANGUAGE OF ORIGINAL DOCUMENT: English
DOCUMENT TYPE: Book

Ramsey, G.P.
Race music: Black cultures from bebop to hip-hop
(2003) Race Music: Black Cultures from Bebop to Hip-Hop, 281 p.
PUBLISHER: University of California Press
LANGUAGE OF ORIGINAL DOCUMENT: English
DOCUMENT TYPE: Book

Dettmar, K.J.H.
Is pranksta rap ready for prime time?
(2003) Chronicle of Higher Education, 49 (27 SEC.2), pp. B16.
LANGUAGE OF ORIGINAL DOCUMENT: English
DOCUMENT TYPE: Article

Stolley, M.R., Fitzgibbon, M.L., Dyer, A., Van Horn, L., KauferChristoffel, K., Schiffer, L.
Hip-Hop to Health Jr., an obesity prevention program for minority preschool children: Baseline characteristics of participants

(2003) Preventive Medicine, 36 (3), pp. 320-329.
   PUBLISHER: Academic Press Inc.
   LANGUAGE OF ORIGINAL DOCUMENT: English
   DOCUMENT TYPE: Article

Alim, H.S.
**On Some Serious Next Millennium Rap Ishhh: Pharoahe Monch,
Hip Hop Poetics, and the Internal Rhymes of Internal Affairs**

(2003) Journal of English Linguistics, 31 (1), pp. 60-84.
LANGUAGE OF ORIGINAL DOCUMENT: English
DOCUMENT TYPE: Article

Androutsopoulos, J., Scholz, A.
Spaghetti funk: Appropriations of hip-hop culture and rap music in europe
(2003) Popular Music and Society, 26 (4), pp. 463-479.
LANGUAGE OF ORIGINAL DOCUMENT: English
DOCUMENT TYPE: Article

Ibrahim, A.
Marking the unmarked: Hip-hop, the gaze & the african body in north america
(2003) Critical Arts, 17 (1-2), pp. 52-70.
LANGUAGE OF ORIGINAL DOCUMENT: English
DOCUMENT TYPE: Article

Templeton, I.H.
Where in the world is the hip hop nation?
(2003) Popular Music, 22 (2), pp. 241-245.
LANGUAGE OF ORIGINAL DOCUMENT: English
DOCUMENT TYPE: Article

Feffer, S.
Extending the breaks: Fires in the mirror in the context of hip-hop structure, style, and culture
(2003) Comparative Drama, 37 (3-4), pp. 397-415.
PUBLISHER: Western Michigan University
LANGUAGE OF ORIGINAL DOCUMENT: English
DOCUMENT TYPE: Article

Iwamoto, D.
Tupac shakur: Understanding the identity formation of hyper-masculinity of a popular hip-hop artist
(2003) Black Scholar, 33 (2), pp. 44-49.
LANGUAGE OF ORIGINAL DOCUMENT: English
DOCUMENT TYPE: Article

Orlando, V.
From rap to raï in the mixing bowl: Beur hip-hop culture and banlieue cinema in urban France
(2003) Journal of Popular Culture, 36 (3), pp. 395-415.
PUBLISHER: Blackwell Publishing Ltd
LANGUAGE OF ORIGINAL DOCUMENT: English
DOCUMENT TYPE: Review

Cutler, C.
"Keepin'it real": White hip-hoppers' discourses of language, race, and authenticity
(2003) Journal of Linguistic Anthropology, 13 (2), pp. 211-233.
LANGUAGE OF ORIGINAL DOCUMENT: English
DOCUMENT TYPE: Article

Mahiri, J., Conner, E.
Black youth violence has a bad rap
(2003) Journal of Social Issues, 59 (1), pp. 121-140.
PUBLISHER: Blackwell Publishing Inc.
LANGUAGE OF ORIGINAL DOCUMENT: English
DOCUMENT TYPE: Article

Yousman, B.
Blackophilia and Blackophobia: White youth, the consumption of rap music, and white supremacy
(2003) Communication Theory, 13 (4), pp. 366-391.
PUBLISHER: Oxford University Press
LANGUAGE OF ORIGINAL DOCUMENT: English
DOCUMENT TYPE: Article

Fernandes, S.
Island paradise, revolutionary utopia or hustler's haven? consumerism and socialism in contemporary cuban rap
(2003) International Journal of Phytoremediation, 21 (1), pp. 359-375.
LANGUAGE OF ORIGINAL DOCUMENT: English
DOCUMENT TYPE: Article

Dawson, A.
'This is the Digital Underclass': Asian Dub Foundation and Hip-Hop Cosmopolitanism
(2002) Social Semiotics, 12 (1), pp. 27-44.
LANGUAGE OF ORIGINAL DOCUMENT: English
DOCUMENT TYPE: Article

Bluher, D.
The «rebus bitches» or the representation of women in the Maghreb French cinema hip-hop [Les «Meufs rebeus» ou la représentation des femmes maghrébines dans le cinéma français hip-hop]
(2002) Esprit Createur, 42 (1), pp. 84-95.
LANGUAGE OF ORIGINAL DOCUMENT: French
DOCUMENT TYPE: Article

Chang, J.
The hip-hop generation can call for peace
(2002) Amerasia Journal, 28 (1), pp. 167-172.
LANGUAGE OF ORIGINAL DOCUMENT: English
DOCUMENT TYPE: Article

Kun, J.
Two turntables and a social movement: Writing hip-hop at century's end
(2002) American Literary History, 14 (3), pp. 580-592.
LANGUAGE OF ORIGINAL DOCUMENT: English
DOCUMENT TYPE: Article

Middleton, J., Beebe, R.
The racial politics of hybridity and 'neo-eclecticism' in contemporary popular music
(2002) Popular Music, 21 (2), pp. 159-172.
LANGUAGE OF ORIGINAL DOCUMENT: English
DOCUMENT TYPE: Article

Rozie-Battle, J.L.

African American youth in the new millennium: An overview
(2002) Journal of Health and Social Policy, 15 (2), pp. 1-12.
LANGUAGE OF ORIGINAL DOCUMENT: English
DOCUMENT TYPE: Review

Peres, C.A., Peres, R.A., Da Silveira, F., Paiva, V., Hudes, E.S., Hearst, N.
Developing an AIDS prevention intervention for incarcerated male adolescents in Brazil
(2002) AIDS Education and Prevention, 14 (5 SUPPL.), pp. 36-44.
LANGUAGE OF ORIGINAL DOCUMENT: English
DOCUMENT TYPE: Article

Aidi, H.
Jihadis in the Hood: Race, urban Islam and the war on terror
(2002) Middle East Report, (224), pp. 36-43.
LANGUAGE OF ORIGINAL DOCUMENT: English
DOCUMENT TYPE: Article

Grassilli, M.
Atzinganoi, mint tea and hip hop: (Multi)cultural education in Bologna

(2002) Studi Emigrazione, (145), pp. 137-159.
LANGUAGE OF ORIGINAL DOCUMENT: Italian
DOCUMENT TYPE: Article

Emerson, R.A.
"Where my girls at?" negotiating Black womanhood in music videos
(2002) Gender and Society, 16 (1), pp. 115-135.
LANGUAGE OF ORIGINAL DOCUMENT: English
DOCUMENT TYPE: Review

Kaya, A.
Aesthetics of diaspora: Contemporary minstrels in Turkish Berlin
(2002) Journal of Ethnic and Migration Studies, 28 (1), pp. 43-62.
LANGUAGE OF ORIGINAL DOCUMENT: English
DOCUMENT TYPE: Article

Fitzgibbon, M.L., Stolley, M.R., Dyer, A.R., VanHorn, L., KauferChristoffel, K.
A community-based obesity prevention program for minority children: Rationale and study design for Hip-Hop to Health Jr.
(2002) Preventive Medicine, 34 (2), pp. 289-297.
PUBLISHER: Academic Press Inc.
LANGUAGE OF ORIGINAL DOCUMENT: English
DOCUMENT TYPE: Article

Ramsey Jr., G.P.
Muzing new hoods, making new identities: Film, hip-hop culture, and jazz music
(2002) Callaloo, 25 (1), pp. 309-320.
PUBLISHER: Johns Hopkins University Press
LANGUAGE OF ORIGINAL DOCUMENT: English
DOCUMENT TYPE: Review

Alim, H.S.
Street-conscious copula variation in the hip hop nation
(2002) American Speech, 77 (3), pp. 288-304.
PUBLISHER: Duke University Press

LANGUAGE OF ORIGINAL DOCUMENT: English
DOCUMENT TYPE: Review

Ma, E.K.-W.
Translocal spatiality
(2002) International Journal of Cultural Studies, 5 (2), pp. 131-152.
LANGUAGE OF ORIGINAL DOCUMENT: English
DOCUMENT TYPE: Article

Watts, R.J., Abdul-Adil, J.K., Pratt, T.
Enhancing Critical Consciousness in Young African American Men. A Psychoeducational Approach
(2002) Psychology of Men and Masculinity, 3 (1), pp. 41-50.
LANGUAGE OF ORIGINAL DOCUMENT: English
DOCUMENT TYPE: Article

Engel, L.
Body poetics of hip hop dance styles in Copenhagen
(2001) Dance Chronicle, 24 (3), pp. 351-372.
LANGUAGE OF ORIGINAL DOCUMENT: English
DOCUMENT TYPE: Article

Basu, D., Werbner, P.
Bootstrap capitalism and the culture industries: A critique of invidious comparisons in the study of ethnic entrepreneurship
(2001) Ethnic and Racial Studies, 24 (2), pp. 236-262.
LANGUAGE OF ORIGINAL DOCUMENT: English
DOCUMENT TYPE: Article

White, S.D., Lester, W.F.
Cultural relevance: Hip-hop music as a bridge to the digital divide
(2001) Proceedings of the Hawaii International Conference on System Sciences, art. no. 26, p. 13.
LANGUAGE OF ORIGINAL DOCUMENT: English
DOCUMENT TYPE: Article

Forman, M.

It ain't all about the benjamins: Summit on social responsibility in the hip-hop industry
(2001) Journal of Popular Music Studies, 13 (1), pp. 117-123.
LANGUAGE OF ORIGINAL DOCUMENT: English
DOCUMENT TYPE: Article

Lenz, M.
Hip-hop landscapes
(2001) Journal of Popular Music Studies, 13 (2), pp. 245-248.
LANGUAGE OF ORIGINAL DOCUMENT: English
DOCUMENT TYPE: Article

Laboskey, S.
Getting Off: Portrayals of Masculinity in Hip Hop Dance in Film
(2001) Dance Research Journal, 33 (2), pp. 112-120.
LANGUAGE OF ORIGINAL DOCUMENT: English
DOCUMENT TYPE: Article

Diessel, C.
Bridging east and west on the "orient express": Oriental hip-hop in the turkish diaspora of berlin
(2001) Journal of Popular Music Studies, 13 (2), pp. 165-187.
LANGUAGE OF ORIGINAL DOCUMENT: English
DOCUMENT TYPE: Article

Watkins, S.C.
A nation of millions: Hip hop culture and the legacy of black nationalism
(2001) Communication Review, 4 (3), pp. 373-398.
LANGUAGE OF ORIGINAL DOCUMENT: English
DOCUMENT TYPE: Article

Olivo, W.
Phat lines: Spelling conventions in rap music
(2001) Written Language and Literacy, 4 (1), pp. 67-85.
LANGUAGE OF ORIGINAL DOCUMENT: English
DOCUMENT TYPE: Article

Lanik, J.

Goal of education: Cultural maturity: Twenty ideas for intercultural education
(2001) European Education, 33 (3), pp. 85-94.
LANGUAGE OF ORIGINAL DOCUMENT: English
DOCUMENT TYPE: Article

Jackson, J.D.
Improvisation in African-American Vernacular Dancing
(2001) Dance Research Journal, 33 (2), pp. 40-53.
LANGUAGE OF ORIGINAL DOCUMENT: English
DOCUMENT TYPE: Article

Chenciner, A., Venturelli, A.
Minima de l'intégrale d'action du problème Newtonien de 4 corps de masses égales dans R3: Orbites 'hip-hop'
(2000) Celestial Mechanics and Dynamical Astronomy, 77 (2), pp. 139-152.
LANGUAGE OF ORIGINAL DOCUMENT: French
DOCUMENT TYPE: Article

Fenn, J., PeruIlo, A.

Language choice and hip hop in Tanzania and Malawi
(2000) Popular Music and Society, 24 (3), pp. 73-93.
LANGUAGE OF ORIGINAL DOCUMENT: English
DOCUMENT TYPE: Article

Bluher, D.
Souviens-toi de moi: A hip-hop film?
(2000) Contemporary French and Francophone Studies, 4 (2), pp. 353-365.
LANGUAGE OF ORIGINAL DOCUMENT: English
DOCUMENT TYPE: Article

Mitchell, T.
Doin' damage in my native language: The use of "resistance vernaculars" in hip hop in France, Italy, and Aotearoa/New Zealand
(2000) Popular Music and Society, 24 (3), pp. 41-54.
LANGUAGE OF ORIGINAL DOCUMENT: English
DOCUMENT TYPE: Article

Smith, S.
STUDENT ARTICLE Compositional strategies of the hip-hop tumtablist
(2000) Organised Sound, 5 (2), pp. 75-79.
LANGUAGE OF ORIGINAL DOCUMENT: English
DOCUMENT TYPE: Article

Wilkins, C.L.
(W)rapped space: The architecture of hip hop
(2000) Journal of Architectural Education, 54 (1), pp. 7-19.
PUBLISHER: Routledge
LANGUAGE OF ORIGINAL DOCUMENT: English
DOCUMENT TYPE: Review

Lang, C.
The new global and urban order: Legacies for the "Hip-Hop Generation"
(2000) Race and Society, 3 (2), pp. 111-142.
PUBLISHER: Elsevier BV

LANGUAGE OF ORIGINAL DOCUMENT: English
DOCUMENT TYPE: Article

Sharma, S., Sharma, A.
'So Far So Good…': La Haine and the Poetics of the Everyday
(2000) Theory, Culture & Society, 17 (3), pp. 103-116.
LANGUAGE OF ORIGINAL DOCUMENT: English
DOCUMENT TYPE: Article

Wright, S.
'A Love Born of Hate': Autonomist Rap in Italy
(2000) Theory, Culture & Society, 17 (3), pp. 117-135.
LANGUAGE OF ORIGINAL DOCUMENT: English
DOCUMENT TYPE: Article

Hutnyk, J., Sharma, S.
Music & Politics: An Introduction
(2000) Theory, Culture & Society, 17 (3), pp. 55-63.
LANGUAGE OF ORIGINAL DOCUMENT: English
DOCUMENT TYPE: Article

Brittin, R.V.
Children's Preference for Sequenced Accompaniments: The Influence of Style and Perceived Tempo
(2000) Journal of Research in Music Education, 48 (3), pp. 237-248.
LANGUAGE OF ORIGINAL DOCUMENT: English
DOCUMENT TYPE: Article

ABOUT THE AUTHOR

Vasileios Yfantis holds 2 Master Degrees in Information Technology and has been working on music since the late 1990s by experimenting with tape mixing and sound design. Billy is playing digital keyboards, but prefers to express his artistic dream through the electronic sounds that come from unusual machines. He has experimented with the recording of vacuum cleaners, electric blenders and other strange sounds that have resulted in musical releases. Moreover, Billy has authored books on music, business and science while from times to times he speaks about the electronic governance at scientific conferences all over Europe.

Bibliography
1. V. Yfantis, "The Commercial Exploitation Of Color As A Consumer Stimulus" (Greek Edition), Createspace, 2013.
2. V. Yfantis, "The Lost Lyrics" (Greek Edition), Createspace, 2013.
3. V. Yfantis, "Punk Goes Science: The Academic Punk Bibliography",CreateSpace, 2014.
4. V. Yfantis, "City Streets Of Europe", Lulu, 2017.
5. V. Yfantis, "Metal Goes Science", Createspace 2017.

Discography
1. Billy Yfantis - The Noisy Whispers Compilation (Full album, 2019)
2. Billy Yfantis - The Mysterious Trip (Digital single, 2018)
3. Billy Yfantis - Dust Not Found (Digital single 2017)
4. Billy Yfantis - Crossing The Line (Digital single 2016)
5. Billy Yfantis - The Electric Blender Session (Digital single, 2016)
6. Billy Yfantis - The Missing Link (Digital single, 2015)

The music is available on the most digital platforms including, Spotify, Tidal, Deezer, iTunes, etc.

Contact: Byfantis@yahoo.com

www.ingramcontent.com/pod-product-compliance
Lightning Source LLC
Chambersburg PA
CBHW031234250726
48655CB00005B/1944